REAL SUPERMAN

The Training Guide to Become
Tougher, Deadlier and More Fearless
than 99% of the Population!

Vol. 2: The Fighting Edition

---

by Markus A. Kassel

Disclaimer: this book is meant for information and educational purposes only. Consult with your physician before attempting any of the exercises described in this book. The author will not be held accountable for any damage caused by the implementation of the advice given throughout this guide. Though the author found success with this method, results may vary from person to person.

First Edition.

Cover image: Copyright © Rangizzz

Visit the author's website: http://RealLifeSuperman.com

Table of Contents

The Fighting Game: Life Is Not a Comic Book, or Is It?

Unbreakable – the movie – is not only a lot of fun and a great hero story; it's become famous for its twist ending where Samuel L. Jackson's character sums up the duality of this world in a few words:

Now that we know who you are", he says to the Indestructible man. *"I know who I am. I'm not a mistake! It all makes sense. In a comic, you know how you can tell who the arch villain's going to be? He's the exact opposite of the hero.*

If you want to be a real life Superman, you will have to deal with a Lex Luthor. An arch nemesis. Because **without villains, there can be no superheroes**. One needs the other in order to exist; they define each other. Like night and day. Good and evil. Jedi Masters and Sith Lords. Mankind and White Walkers...

Which means that, sooner or later, fights will arise. And if you may nip some in the bud with an imposing build (courtesy of **Real Life Superman – Volume 01**), it's only a matter of time before you end up having to defend yourself or someone else. It only takes once, just like with first aid. But if you don't know what to do come that crucial time, it could cost you dearly. And yes, I'm talking about your life! Learning how to fight is a necessity for anyone, especially if your goal is to become all you can be.

When I was a kid, I thought that – to get rid of someone – all you had to do was slap him Batman-style. I was reading too many comics and thought we were living in a world where fighting was a harmless game, a bit like cops & robbers; that it was all pretending and faking. After my first Karate class and kick to the guts, I found out that it wasn't so!

I learned that not only fists hurt, and that they do worse than skinning your knees and biting the dust, you can't get rid of someone as easily as in the movies. People won't just drop like flies at your mere sight; they're resilient and they will keep coming back unless you take them out cold on the spot.

Fighting another human being is not like sparring with a punching bag. Your target will dodge your blows, make feints and hit back! It will not just stand there for you to swing at, unless you pay him good money!

I'm not going to detail my whole story again; my many setbacks, trials & errors on this journey to a superior body. If you've read my previous book, you already know everything about me but the color of my briefs (ha ha, I tricked you. I wear boxers!) What those Karate lessons taught me, though, was that to develop into a great fighter, I had to broaden my horizons.

The more I learned about this art, the more I realized that Karate by itself would never get me where I needed to be. It provided a nice basis from which to draw from but it was too fancy for its own good. Katas looked as smooth and beautiful as dance choreographies but, in the end, they were about just as effective in a real brawl situation!

Sorry kiddo but Karate won't do! (Markus aged 3)

As I read about other disciplines and moved up the ranks from white belt to black, its shortcomings were becoming more and more obvious. Punches with the hands on the hips left your body completely open to counterattacks. Blocking techniques a la Karate Kid were a big joke and the fighting stances not dynamic enough. But what really left me grinding my teeth was the spirit that pervaded the club.

Don't get me wrong, I can understand that every martial arts practitioner on planet Earth isn't looking to become the next Iron Fist and that there must be room for easier, less hardcore training methods... but this was just too nicey-nicey, too family friendly. Not rough enough. People went there to exercise like they would an aerobics class. They wanted to work out and have a good time. Not become better fighters.

To sum things up, it left me unprepared, with too many holes in my game. Here was a 1st degree black belt who would get his butt handed to him in a bar clash if he had to face a guy with any type of real fight experience! My belt was worthless, except for holding my trousers of course. I still had so much to learn...

This book is the result of every drop of sweat I shed, every questioning and wince of pain I subjected myself to in the years that followed. It's the condensed reflection of all the knowledge I acquired on the most effective methods to develop your fighting skills.

As a training guide, it can be read as a standalone which should provide you with everything you need to reach your objectives. That is actionable techniques to make you more elusive and powerful. But it bears mentioning that this series is supposed to be read in order as each volume builds upon the previous issue; so, if you can, make sure you read "book 01" dedicated to strength & conditioning prior to this, to get in sufficient shape to make the most of this new material.

Get in shape first!

The "Real Life Superman" system is a comprehensive program. It's not only designed to turn you into a lethal weapon; it aims to make you as well-rounded as possible by working on every critical part of your mind, body and soul. We want a strong and muscular physique that's as explosive as it is resilient but we also want a spirit of steel that's quick, sophisticated and indomitable. In short, we want it all!

As we did in the first installment, we will only deal with the best, most efficient training drills here; the exercises that will make you tougher, deadlier and more fearless by the week! I'll share my every secret to bring you to the top of the food chain.

If you've already gone through my first "100 days program", you should now have cultivated one fit body which strikes by its stamina and agility. Let's see how to bring it to the next level and **make it invincible**!

6 Steps to Go from Victim to Killing Machine

When you think about it, there are almost as many ways to fight as there are superheroes in the Marvel universe. Which is bad news for the newbie in search of a club to join. From the most famous to the most obscure martials arts and combat sports, you've got Judo, Boxing, Capoeira, Kung fu, Aikido, Jiu jitsu, Tai chi, Hapkido, Wrestling, Krav-maga, Taekwondo, Viet-vo-dao, Full-contact, Muay thai, Pencak silat, Sambo, Jeet kune do, and a whole bunch of others you've probably never heard of (Kino mutai, anyone???)

Even within each one of those disciplines, you have a huge number of contrasting schools. Shaolin Kung fu, Kyokushinkai Karate, Brazilian Jiu jitsu... And let's not get started on personal styles and their impact on the way different people will fight!

How is one supposed to make sense of this mess? Can you pick one at random and consider it as valid a choice as the next one? As I hinted in the introduction with my foray into Karate, if you want to take up a new sport to get in shape and feel better, please be my guest and let the gods decide for you. But if you're after a training method that will offer you the tools to face any danger or life-threatening situation, I'm sorry to break it to you: you'll have more chance of winning the lottery than stumbling upon the right pony!

"OK, I got it!" you say. "Tell me already what to do then, Markus!" Getting impatient there, mate, aren't we? I want you to understand my train of thought to see where I'm coming from...

You know, trying to organize those divergent views would quickly give us a headache anyway. There are too many ways to categorize them; by separating those putting the emphasis on grappling and chokes from those that favor striking, for example, or by relating them to their country of origin. A better alternative in my opinion would be not to judge each art separately but to focus on the particular techniques they all teach.

When you break them down to their bare essentials, you'll find lots of similarities at their core. There will obviously be nuances and subtleties in the way they're performed but, in essence, they will remain quite close. Our job will thus be to discriminate between them according to 2 factors: **beauty and efficiency**. In the world of fighting, it seems like those variables represent the 2 sides of the same coin. Like the rifle and the gun in Full Metal Jacket's song: one's for fighting, the other's for fun.

As a big fan of Jet Li, Jackie and other masters of the flashy (if you are as well, Google "martial arts tricking" and get ready to have your mind blown away), I'm really sad to say this but the prettier a technique, the less effective it usually is. Like those flying kicks heroes throw in the movies and which prove to be as useful in real life as a slap with a fly swatter. Our goal isn't to learn how to wow bystanders with back flips but to get the job done quickly and with incurring as little damage as possible. Therefore, all the nice spinning and acrobatic stuff will be discarded. Yes, you can weep now.

This is serious business. If I'm to honor the same promise I kept in volume 01 where I made you faster, stronger and more jacked than 99% of the population, we need to stick to the other extreme of the spectrum and favor efficiency over beauty. To get an idea of our present situation and the road still ahead of us, let's put things in perspective first: where are those 99% of people we're trying to "beat" on the prowess scale?

Most of the population never learned to protect itself properly; it's a fact. If we, as humans, have many inborn abilities, and defending ourselves against predators might be one of them, it doesn't mean that it comes out gracefully when it must. Have you ever watched two regular guys go at each other? Swinging their arms without aim as if they were drowning? It's so bad it's funny.

And those who did "train" to fight, they often did so by following the same useless process I was bad-mouthing a few paragraphs back. They think their *yama-tsukis* are going to save the day if they ever get in trouble but the truth is that they're as vulnerable as the next guy. They never learned to take a good hit and, more often than not, they just won't be ready to handle the fear and adrenalin rush once they'll be facing a real threat. We've got our work cut out for us.

To rise above the rest, we'll need to cover all bases by preparing you both physically and mentally. Here are the different parts we'll go through during this program:

- **Part I – Fighting Basics: Building Your Arsenal**: this will be the most critical part of this book, that from which all the others derive. I'll show you the best stance to adopt to both protect your vital organs and move efficiently, and the appropriate technique to deliver kicks and punches;
- **Part II – Speed Kills: Strike like Lightning**: without speed, you might as well lie down in front of your opponent and let him do as he pleases. It's crucial not only to close the distance and manage to land strikes but also to avoid getting hit yourself. Here, I'll show you how to increase your velocity with a few easy drills but also what stretching exercises to perform to improve your flexibility;
- **Part III – Power Training & Body Strengthening: Develop a Tough Skin and Sledgehammers for Fists**: to learn the secret behind massive power that would have nothing to envy to Hulk's, this is where it happens. We'll also see how you can train your body to withstand pain and make it as hard as a rock;
- **Part IV – The Psychology of Fighting: Tame the Fear and Get the Upper Hand**: as they say, it's all in the head; the place that can make a heaven of hell and a hell of heaven. In this chapter, I'll show you how to get prepared for any confrontation and avoid letting fear get the best of you;
- **Part V – Advanced Fighting Techniques: Anything Goes**: dealing with multiple adversaries and weapons, attacking with the head, the elbows and the knees, training your situational awareness... Those are some of the areas we'll work on here;
- **Part VI – The 100 Days Program to Make a Killer out of You**: without a program, this guide would do you as much good as a romance novel. You'd just read it, nod in a few places, then toss it in a corner and forget about it. The plan I'll lay out in Part VI will ensure you take action and take the first steps towards your transformation.

Alright my friend, warm those knuckles up, crack your neck, and let's get ready to rumble! You're only 100 days away from becoming tougher, deadlier and more powerful than 99% of the population!

PART I

Fighting Basics: Building Your Arsenal

"To successfully make a shot,
you gotta follow and master basic steps.
Your stance is the foundation.
Where you draw your strength."

Hawkeye

Choosing the Right Stance

First things first, before I teach you to throw down, we need to make sure you're standing correctly. A good stance is critical in that it can either hinder your speed, power, defense and ability to strike. Or facilitate them. As with the extensive range of martial arts available, dozens of stances exist with a great deal looking straight out of a bad Kung Fu movie.

The perfect fighting posture should tick all the following boxes:

- Protect our vulnerable areas, namely the face (jaw, temples, eyes), the neck, the groin and the ribcage;
- Allow us to move fluidly, to jump out of harm's way and dodge a hit. Or to come in like thunder and deliver our own brand of punishment;
- Give us an optimal reach for every limb;
- Provide us with strong footing and a solid balance;
- Ease the transfer of power from our body to the point of impact.

I've found that the best compromise to meet those criteria would be to adopt a modified Muay thai stance. A hard hitting sport that makes extensive use of knees and elbows, Thai boxing has evolved a very strong guard in the five centuries that it's been conquering the rings all over the globe. With a few tiny changes to our feet position to allow for more dynamic motions, it will maximize our strengths while protecting most of our weaknesses.

From top to bottom, here are the key points to watch out for:

Head position

Want a one-way ticket for the floor and the land of unconsciousness? Easy! Leave your head up and your chin exposed. You'll be eating dirt in no time! The perfect head position is bent forward just enough to tuck the chin and protect your jaw. Never tilt it backward, even to avoid a strike. That's how people get knocked out.

Arms Position

The arms will play a backup role to the head, but their job is as important for offense as it is for defense. Forget about the usual Karate stance with one hand at your hip and the other straightened in front of your groin as if to say "no, not the family jewels!" Your hands will be kept where they belong; high at face level, with the right stuck to your chin if you're right-handed and the left a few inches before your nose (or the other way around if you're a leftie.)

That way, your hands will be able to further protect your sensible spots like the bridge of your nose and your temples. With the hands in that position, you will also block punches more easily and absorb their power by ducking your head inside your forearms. Or strike much faster as your fists will only have a short distance to travel to reach your opponent's ugly mug.

As far as the elbows are concerned, you will need to keep them close to your ribcage. They're the shield to your ribs, sternum and abs, but they also keep you safe from liver shots which may take you out like a hammer blow from our dear Thor. So, never flare them.

Your shoulders will provide protection from the sides; they'll represent your lateral airbags. If you want to lift them up to help your chin hide inside your guard, try and leave them relaxed. Putting too much tension in your shoulders and upper back would prove detrimental to your speed by making you too stiff. And it would also exhaust you far faster. Finally, turn your shoulders slightly to your dominant side, along with your trunk, to offer your enemy a smaller target.

Torso Position

There's not much to say here. Like I told you, turn sideways, but not so much that it would start impeding your movements; a few degrees should suffice. Engage your abs to help with your reaction time. You see, your core is at the origin of most movements. By keeping it readied, you'll guarantee yourself a greater adaptability. Holding a light contraction in the abdominals will also protect your internal organs in case you do get hit in the gut.

Legs & Feet Position

For the legs, it's important to keep the knees bent. Those will act like springs by cushioning any shock, allowing your body to move quickly in any direction and change heights with ease.

Along with that of your hands, the placement of your feet is the most critical part of a good stance. For one, you will want to arrange them at a slight angle, shoulder-width apart, and pointing towards your dominant side.

Then, you'll want to make sure you don't stay flat footed as you would become a sitting duck. Rest on the balls of your feet, especially with the back leg.

As far as weight distribution goes, spread it equally on both feet. Putting too much weight on the front leg will make you heavy and slow. Resting on the back leg, on the other hand, will rob you of your power and get you unbalanced.

Punching Techniques

Now that we know how to position ourselves for maximum efficiency, let's see how to turn those clumsy paws of yours into weapons of mass destruction. In a fight situation, punching techniques will represent your main offensive tool. Though you may choose to strike with the palm of your hands, their edge, or the tip of your fingers, I suggest you put those fancy options to the side.

For many reasons, your hands are at their strongest with a clenched fist. For one, it gives them extreme versatility by allowing them to strike from any position or angle, and to do it without losing any power. It offers good penetration as well and a certain degree of protection to your bones and articulations.

By making your hands one compact mass, you reduce the risk of injury. I can't stress enough how it sucks to break a hand in the middle of a fight and being unable to use it anymore! That's why we'll learn in Part III how to strengthen your fists like those guys who get a kick out of breaking bricks.

But let's not digress. Back to the subject at hand: boxing moves. I'll tell you right away, we won't have a hundred different techniques to work on and memorize. It's better to study a few moves and become very proficient at them than to know twice as many but to execute them with a poor and sloppy form.

As the great Bruce Lee once said: *I fear not the man who has practiced 10,000 kicks once, but I fear the man who has practiced one kick 10,000 times*. Practice makes perfect... but only when focusing on a handful of techniques. Anyway, there are only a couple strikes worth our time. And you know what? You're in luck as those are exactly the ones we'll deal with here! What a beautiful coincidence, isn't it?

The first moves to train will be:

The Jab & the Cross

To throw a jab, standing in the regular fighting stance we just described, turn your hips to the right and extend your left hand in front of you in a straight line. Perform the movement as fast and with as much power as possible. Make it snap. Try not to telegraph your move; start the jab without any loading, right from your hand's position in the guard. Keep the chin tucked and the shoulders in protection. Come back to your starting point after the full extension.

The jab is a great weapon which is often underused. Even by those few who do know how to scrap. People will often resort to rights and hooks, relegating the jab to a second zone technique, weak and ineffective, whose sole purpose is to open a combination.

They might not end a bout with a single strike but... jabs CAN do damage. They CAN break your adversary's will and make him quit. It's all a question of good delivery and timing. Throw it stiff while the guy's rushing towards you, and it'll be like he smashed his face into a wall. Drill it. Drill it. Drill it!

The right or cross, on the other hand, represents your main dealer of KOs. It starts from further away than the jab (thus, allowing for more speed to build) and benefits from your stronger side. Therefore, it comes with much more power. When it lands clean on the chin, it's usually good night.

To execute that technique, it's a bit like the previous one but in reverse. Turn your hips to the left. Unload your strike straight and make a slight pivot with the rear foot to further engage the hips and realign the rest of your body.

The Hook

Hooks have a shorter range than straight punches as your arms will be bent at the elbow during the move. But what they lack in reach, they make up for with power. They pack a punch, if you allow me the pun!

Unlike the previous techniques, with hooks your shoulders won't do much work and neither will your triceps. Hooks are all about the hips. You will raise your striking arm and lift the elbow so that your forearm is parallel to the floor and the angle between biceps and radius about 45 degrees. Then, rotate your hips and foot to the side you want to throw your blow to and your hand will follow the motion. Make sure to keep your elbow locked for maximum power and to prevent it from extending and causing injury.

The Uppercut

I'm not a big fan of uppercuts because their use is quite limited but they can be extremely effective in close range to surprise your enemy. Because of the angle at which they strike, uppercuts will often come unnoticed until they actually land. And, as they say, it's the one hit you don't see coming that knocks you down! So...

It will also provide some diversity to your punches and keep the adversary guessing. Like I said, uppercuts are an upward movement. To do one, you will have to involve your hips once again. For a left uppercut, bend the knees and turn your torso and hips to the left. This is important because your hips have to drop low in order to get any pizazz off that punch. Then, rotate the hips to the right while driving your left hand and shoulder vertically. Push with your lead leg to generate even more power.

Unlike straights and hooks, uppercuts are seldom used as a one-shot. Nothing prevents you from launching a combination with one, especially if your foe is pressed against a wall or cornered. But beware because uppercuts will leave you open to counterattacks at that brief moment when you twist sideways to load your hips and let your guard down.

That's one of the reasons why I don't use them much. And if I do, I'll use them after a cross or a hook, not to have to "load" as much.

That's it as far as basic punches go. I know, this list is quite on the short side and you're eager to learn as much as possible, but you don't really need anything else to get the job done and to have it done well. Spinning back fists will only have you lose your advantage and give a chance to the other guy to unleash his fury on you. As for Superman punches... Ah, Superman punches! Though you can probably imagine how much I would have loved to include that technique in our program – a superhero attack for supermen in the making; how cool would that have been, huh? –, like I said, we're not here to please the crowd. If you want to learn jaw-dropping moves that will not only have people worship you but that will also build your strength beyond your wildest dreams, I'll see you back in volume 05 of this series that will deal with expert level power moves like the planche and the human flag. But here, we want efficiency. Not beauty.

So, drill those 3 techniques. Make them the very basis of your training. Grow intimate with them. Visit them time and time again, until they become as natural to you as breathing.

Kicking Techniques

When the time comes to select the best kicks to study, the matter gets even more complicated. The tricky part about kicks is that, by definition, as one of your feet leaves the floor to meet and greet your adversary's soft spots, you give up one of your support points. It's like sacrificing a rook or board position in chess in hopes of getting closer to a chess mate. It can backfire and, next thing you know, you're on your back with fists raining down on your face like meteorites on apocalypse day.

If you follow combat sports, you know that kicks leading to a knock-out are a rarity compared to punches (that's why they're the main attraction of a fighter's highlight reel when someone managed to end a bout with one.) That's not to say that they're useless; in fact, it would be quite the opposite. I'm just saying that we'll have to be careful with them not to make a mistake we could regret later.

The Low Kick

The first, and also my favorite, leg technique to learn is the low kick. While your punches aim to send your rival to la la land, low kicks aka leg kicks will play another but no less important role. They'll work as a sapping technique like the blows of a lumberjack, hitting and hitting that tree with his axe until it finally comes tumbling down.

By digging your shin into the thighs of Mr. Bad Guy, over and over again, you will rob him of his ability to move. Because of the pain he'll feel every time he steps on his bruised leg, he won't be able to put much weight on it anymore. Which will make his movements slower and his strikes much weaker. Nice tool to add to your arsenal, isn't it?

To throw a regular leg kick, lift your rear foot off the ground, turn your hips to the side you're attacking, and aim with the upper part of your shin towards your opponent's thigh, right above the knee. When your leg makes contact, the bent between your thigh and your shin should be about 90°, and it should travel horizontally like a scythe cutting through wheat.

You can also decide to attack the inside of the leg. The technique will differ slightly and will not come with as much power, but the inner thigh is softer than the outer leg with less muscle mass; so your opponent will feel it for sure!

For an inside leg kick, raise your lead foot and crash it in the area above the knee. Contrary to the outer leg kick, this technique will not land with your leg at a 90° angle. As you're kicking with your front leg, it will be almost entirely extended as it reaches its destination. Also, it won't come totally horizontal either as the distance to travel is much shorter.

Like the uppercut, the leg kick can be thrown on its own but it works best in combinations.

The Middle & the High Kick

The high kick is as close to a cool looking technique as we'll get in this book. Yeah, don't get so excited! It's basically the same motion as a leg kick but targeting the head, though most people won't be able to strike horizontally as it requires extreme flexibility. Because of that, most people will also find that it's their foot or toes that connect with their target and not their shin. The only solution to those problems is to stretch and improve your flexibility (for tips on how to do that, all the way to the full split, meet me back in Part II.)

I consider the high kick sort of a secret weapon. It's best used sparingly for several reasons. For one, your foot being in the air for a longer period of time will increase the risk of you getting thrown off balance. So, don't tempt fate by launching one on every combination. For two, high kicks require more energy and will thus tire you faster than other types of strikes. But mostly, they're best left as a surprise attack that may end fights. When you've already pampered the thighs of your "friend" with some hard leg kicks, he'll have a tendency to reach down with his hands to try and grab/block your leg next time he sees you initiating a kick.

That's when to unload one. Change levels and hit him in the head instead, and watch his eyes freeze in utter terror as his skull goes rolling a couple feet further away. Flawless Victory!

I consider the middle kick another good sapping technique. Where we try to limit an adversary's mobility with leg kicks, here we'll try to take the breath out of him. By targeting the waist and the ribs, we're shooting for extremely sensitive parts that can break and send a thug crying back to his mama.

Another point to stress out with kicking techniques, whichever they are, is to never let your own guard down. Because you're on the offensive, doesn't mean that the other guy will just stand there and wait for you to finish before he gets his turn to taste blood. He might fight back with a punch that, if you dropped your hands to kick, may come and say hello to your chin. So, always exercise caution when using your legs.

The Front Kick

The front kick is one of the most versatile kicking techniques around. It can be used to either push your enemy back and get some room to breathe. Or to attack the stomach and solar plexus to suck the oxygen out of him as with a middle kick.

Usually, the pushing variant to keep someone at bay will be performed with your lead leg. When your opponent steps forward, raise your knee in front of you until your thigh is parallel to the ground. Then, strike with the ball of your foot while pulling backwards with the hips to give power to the kick.

For the stronger version, you'll be using the back leg instead. Make sure to return to your fighting stance once the kick has landed (or missed.) You DON'T want to leave it hanging in the air for the taking. If your kick lacks speed or is too telegraphed, your adversary will have no trouble getting a hold of your leg. Also, if you happen to fight barefoot, watch out for those toes! In all likelihood, you'll be wearing shoes when the battle erupts, so you'll be protected... but I'd suggest training your front kicks barefoot just in case, to teach you to retract those toes when striking and avoid having them crushed. Always be ready for whatever, right?

As far as kicks go, I know most "experts" recommend learning the side kick as well but I consider it to be a poor man's front kick. It can't offer you anything that the front kick can't. It's much slower, as you need to turn sideways to throw it, more easily blocked, very inaccurate, and not that effective anyway. So don't waste your time with it; your efforts will be better spent elsewhere. With straight punches, leg kicks or speed drills, for example.

Then you have all the other kicks, from the axe kick to the *ushiro geri,* but you know what I think about these. Not worth it!

Dodging & Blocking Techniques

Muhammad Ali put it best with his famous quote: *float like a butterfly, sting like a bee. The hands can't hit what the eyes can't see.*

If you want to come in hard when you attack and make your strikes count, you also want to be moving all the time to be as elusive as possible. The best way to defend oneself is not to block or absorb. Having a strong stance can only take you so far. The best way to defend oneself is to move so swiftly that your opponent doesn't even know where to strike! By standing still, you would give him a fixed target that he could reach even if Chong Li had sprayed him with his magical powder. Work on your footwork. Work on your rhythm.

But jumping up and down and changing directions requires a lot of stamina and agility. If you've followed the program detailed in book 01, you should have enough condition already to sustain a good pace. If you haven't, don't worry; we'll see in Part II – dedicated to speed training – and VI – where we'll lay out our 100 days plan to a tougher you – how to get there gradually.

Now that we've gotten that out of the way, let's see exactly what to train to avoid getting your beautiful face rearranged.

Dodging Attacks

Dodging methods follow the principle we just described: relying on your movements to get out of the way, whether it be using your legs, your head or your torso. Their main benefit is that they allow you to stay very close to your opponent, so you can counterattack right away.

The main dodging techniques to escape punches are:

The Layback

This technique is as easy as they come. When you see a straight or hook coming in, bend the rear leg to go back a few inches, out of reach. This is efficiency at its best; moving away just enough to avoid punishment. Good.

The layback will prove especially useful if you're rather on the tall side as ducking (as we'll see below) might not work so well for you if you're still over 6 feet when crouching.

The Punch Slip

Same idea as before but, instead of going backwards to dodge, you will move to the side, left or right depending on the attack. The important point to remember is that you want to slip OUTSIDE the punch. So if you're dealing with a right cross, you'll turn to the left. And the other way around with a jab.

Also, note that it's the entire body that pivots to the side, not just the head or the trunk. Bending at the waist, for example, would severely impede your power and balance. To slip a punch correctly, bend the knees so as to get lower as you pivot, and rotate your body to the side while keeping your eyes on the prize.

Ducking Punches

This time, we're going under the punch. Bend at the knees, just enough to avoid getting hit, while paying attention not to drop too low and sacrificing mobility. Don't bend your back like so many people do; keep it straight.

Also, watch out for any incoming knee that could hurt you on your way down.

Dodging Kicks

As the reach of kicks is greater than that of punches, dodging them usually requires a bounce back or to the side. Which stresses, once again, the importance of being light on your feet and working on your speed.

With that being said, the same techniques used for dodging punches can typically be applied to kicks, but you've got to exercise even more caution. You need to have your distances pinned down to the nearest centimeter to attempt one! To be effective a dodge should see you move just enough to get out of the maimer's trajectory but not so much that you end up losing precious ground. Sometimes, it's a matter of millimeters. If you miscalculated your move, despite your rotation, you might still get hit at high speed. And with a high kick, it's going to hurt!

That's why I want to warn you before we close this section. Dodging and slipping strikes can be a dangerous game. There's always a risk of getting clocked. Training your reflexes will be crucial in your ability to successfully evade attacks, but don't base all your defense around it. Learn to block as well.

Blocking Attacks

In this category, we'll include the moves for both blocking and parrying attacks. The difference between the two is that one will use a strong part of your body as a shield to protect your weaker parts from the blows while the other will merely try and deflect their trajectory away from you.

They each have their pros and cons but deserve to be trained equally so that you always have something to fall back on depending on the situation. Contrary to our offensive moves that we must keep to a minimum to ensure maximum efficiency, for defensive techniques it's better to have more options. As you weather a flurry of punches, you get in a more passive role and can't always use your favorite moves as would be the case with an offense. You might get thrown off balance or find yourself unable to react fast enough to duck under. You will need to deal with that assault any way you can. That's where having an extended range of defensive methods will come in handy and improve your chances of leaving the scene without suffering too much damage.

Now, that doesn't mean that we'll go crazy here and vent the frustration we got from being unable to learn flying kicks by studying every blocking technique there is like the *age uke* and other stupid moves which offer zero protection. Our goal remains unchanged: to become as deadly and tough as we possibly can!

The Shoulder Roll

The shoulder roll can be considered a mix between dodging and blocking. As you see a punch approaching, you will simply roll your shoulders to the other side (in other words, rotate your torso) so that it gets deflected by your arm and doesn't land square on your face. It allows for quick and piercing counters as you don't need to use your hands to deal with the blow.

The shoulder roll is not to be confused with "rolling with a punch" which is a technique where you'll be taking the punch in the head but will turn your neck in the same direction the attack is coming from so that much of its power is taken away. That's the best way to eat a punch if you can neither dodge nor block it. The fist will make contact at full extension instead of at three-quarters which is where it's at its most dangerous. Thus, it won't hurt as much.

The Double Arm Block

For kicks and punches that come straight at your face, you can use the double arm block which is nothing more than bringing your forearms together in front of you for protection. For a successful block, you want to raise your fists – palms facing you – until they reach your eyebrows and contract your arms as the strike lands. As always, don't close your eyes or lift your chin up. Keep focused on your adversary and never compromise on your guard.

The One Arm Block

This one is for blocking circular attacks to the head like hooks and high kicks. Bring one elbow up to the side and rotate with the strike to lessen the impact. Watch out for feints that would leave your ribs exposed.

The Parry

Parrying a strike, as we hinted above, is to deflect its course so as to avoid getting hit. It can be performed with the hand or the forearm, and works for straight punches like the jab and the cross. It's not of much use for hooks and uppercuts because you can't as easily change their trajectory without slamming your own hands in your face.

Once again, this technique will start with a rotation of the hips. If you're parrying the cross of an orthodox fighter, push with your front leg and rotate to the right while using your lead hand to drive the punch away to the inside. In fact, you want to do more than diverting it, you want to push if not slap it aside.

For a jab, you'll parry with the rear hand and turn to the left.

The Leg Kick Check

The main defense against a low kick, if you can't dodge it, is to raise your knee up at an angle and to block it using your own shin. It's also possible to check with the knee instead but it's much harder to achieve because you're trying to block with a much smaller surface. But if you succeed, believe me, your opponent will think twice before he throws another kick!

Checking, however, will not be a pleasant affair. Whether you're the one on the receiving end or the one getting checked. It WILL hurt; that's why it's important to try and elude the kick whenever possible and use yours in combinations to make sure they're not blocked by the other guy. And also to harden your shins so that they become less sensitive. For that last chunk, I'll show you how to do it in Part III.

The Kick Swipe

To deal with a font or side kick, you will use the arm opposite the attacking leg to throw it off to the side with a swipe. This is an interesting technique in that your adversary will find himself off balance, his body facing sideways. Counter with a combination of your own.

Alright, this was a lot of information to absorb in one sitting. Good job, mate! You know now how to stand properly, what attacks to focus on and a few handy moves to save your skin and prevail most of the time.

For any of those techniques to be truly effective though, you still need to develop your speed. If you're as slow as a bimbo checking out the luxury bags on the first day of summer sales, none of those tips will matter. You won't be able to hit your target and you won't move in time to avoid his own strikes.

You've got to become as fast as the Flash. And this is how to do it...

PART II

Speed Kills: Strike like Lightning

*"You're fast, Tony. Very fast.
But I'm always going to be
two seconds ahead of you.
You can set your clock by it."*

Sentry

It will be no grand revelation to learn that, if we had our say in it, it'd be much better to have both speed and power. But if I could only develop one of the two, I'd take speed over power any day. When you match the two and let them fight for it, speed will almost always come out victorious. Not only because of the many reasons already detailed above but also because, in a sense, speed is ALSO power.

You remember Einstein's most celebrated formula? No, not his space cake recipe; I'm talking about $E = MC^2$. If you've never been good with numbers or never really bothered to ponder its signification, it just means that energy (or power in the present case) can be calculated by multiplying an object's mass by the square of the speed at which it's travelling. In other words, increasing your speed is the best thing you could possibly do to improve your power. Where you only have limited control over your weight (mass), with the right exercises you can more than double your speed, which will translate into a gain of energy released at impact not equal to 200% but 400%, thanks to Mr. square!

You're starting to see where we're going with this, little grasshopper? Achieving extreme speed will sit at the top of our list. However, to get there, we'll need to take all its components into account and train them equally. When you dig further, you discover that speed – as far as fighting is concerned – can be expressed in different manners but that it's also dependent on several factors.

On one side, speed is your ability to move – yourself or a part of you – quickly from point A to point B; that would be the quickness of your footwork and your strikes. Then, you have reflexes, which are really nothing more than your speed of reaction. Finally, strength and flexibility will also have their role to play as they can either promote or hinder your velocity.

With the training we undertook in book 01, we've already developed a good basis not only for strength but explosiveness. As I told you back then, they would help us acquire further skills much faster and much more easily. This is where I keep that promise!

We'll need to complement our efforts with specific drills though. Unfortunately, one type of speed does not necessarily translate to another. Being fast at throwing a baseball won't make you a rapid puncher for sure. Speed, much to our dismay, usually is movement specific. We'll need to drill every punching and kicking technique we've seen on top of introducing methods to improve your footwork.

But before we get to these exercises per say, let's see exactly what speed is and how one is supposed to go about improving it on a physiological level.

What It Takes to Enhance Speed

To become quick and sharp with a movement, you have to take 2 important variables under control: quality & frequency. Before you head out into the woods with your ninja outfit and start punching trees and jumping around as if you were Naruto's long lost brother, you ought to focus on quality of motion.

There is no use in trying to build your speed for any given technique if you haven't mastered its mechanics yet. If it takes hundreds and hundreds of repetitions to learn a new movement, it takes THOUSANDS of them to correct a faulty one! So make sure you've got your move down to a T before you drill it and make it a habit! Practice slowly with good form. Patience here, more than ever, will be a saving virtue.

Once you've got the sequence down and perfected, then and only then can you start drilling the technique by increasing its speed. It's only with a high number of repetitions, spaced in time, that you'll be able to become a model of quickness. In a way, it works a little like cramming for school; when you want to store new material in your long-term memory, you need to repeat that info a lot and on several different instances. Going through it 2 or 3 times at once will usually not suffice.

You must strengthen the brain-muscle connections which, with each reinforcement, will make it easier for you to perform the motion in question. Little by little, it will require less concentration on your part and less energy. Without going into too much detail, this will be due to the myelination of the axons involved in the technique you practice. As you keep pounding it, the particular neural pathway concerned will develop a certain type of sheath made of what is called "myelin" and which will allow electrical impulses to travel much faster from one synapse to the other.

Next time your brain launches an order to punch, your body will react more quickly and more efficiently. Energy losses will decline as your technique grows smoother. Eventually, you should also feel more relaxed throughout (though you might have to make a conscious effort to loosen up at first.) Stiffness is often amongst the lead reasons why martial arts and combat sports practitioners never manage to reach a satisfying level of speed. They contract their entire arms to strike; their neck and shoulder girdle are so tight you could almost break a hand patting them on their back...

All that strain works against them by preventing the right muscles from operating at their optimal range. In the best case scenario, muscles should only get tensed the second your fist or foot makes contact with your target. Not before. Think about it as you train and become more proficient.

Alright, time to sum things up: the key to enhance the speed of your attacks is thus to repeat and repeat them with perfect form until they become ingrained and you can execute them without having to think about it. Once you've reached that point, you can start working on making them faster and faster.

If strict form represents an absolute prerequisite, it also means that using ankle or wrist weights to train your speed will not work to your advantage. I can understand why you could think that; after all, if you practice your movements with added weight until you get used to it, once you take it off, you should feel much lighter and therefore be able to throw your attacks with increased ferociousness, right? Sorry but it just ain't so.

The problem is that those weights will change the mechanics of your moves. When you punch with a 5 or 10lbs strap attached to your wrist, your body will not go through the exact same motions as if you had punched without. You'll have to activate certain muscle groups to keep your arm up that wouldn't have been as solicited otherwise; your balance and proprioception will be impacted... In short, it would only serve to confuse your muscles and teach them a wrong way to run. Do that for any extended length of time and you'll have developed one terrible manner you won't be able to rid yourself of!

Like we said, speed is situational. To get better at moving our feet and our body as a whole, we can't solely rely on MetCons, strength building and plyometrics. We need to train specifically for this!

Remember what we said in Part I about the perfect stance? As much as possible, you'll want to avoid standing flat footed. Staying on the balls of your feet will allow for much quicker and fluid motions. It will allow you to come in and out like a shadow, as if you hadn't budged at all. You'll throw your enemy off guard as you change rhythms and he finds himself unable to read your next move.

Yes, footwork is one of the key ingredients to getting the upper hand. And polishing ours will be the main aim of this section.

First things first, now that we've learned to stand correctly – with our hands up, chin down, knees flexed, shoulders relaxed and eyes looking straight ahead –, where do we go from here? How do we move from that position?

If walking is not forbidden per say as it has its uses (to change your pace and give your opponent something more to think about, for example), it's too slow to be effective for offense or defense. Most of the time, we'll be bouncing on the balls of our feet, from left to right, front to back. But much like dancing, to be smooth with your steps, you need to train them diligently. The best way to go about it is by using a jumping rope.

The Many Benefits of the Jumping Rope

If the pull-up bar is the one essential piece of equipment for building a strong upper body, the jumping rope is the one critical tool for achieving a world-class footwork worthy of Ali.

No other device will help improve your coordination, conditioning and agility like a jumping rope will. Moreover, it will teach your legs to move with quick and energetic bursts. Rapid contractions that keep you light on your feet, barely touching the ground, and ready to explode in a snap. And it will make your legs stronger. What else could we ask for?

In one word, it's the ultimate weapon to add to a fighter's arsenal.

Training with a jumping rope is no rocket science. It's as basic as they come; grab it by the handles, make a rotation, and jump as the rope reaches the top of your feet. But if the movement is simple to understand, it doesn't mean that it's easy to put into practice. For the beginner, the challenge will be to manage a few jumps without catching his feet in the rope. This will be the most difficult part. I know, you will feel clumsy at first and want to throw the darn rope out the window, but don't worry. With a little practice, you'll soon be able to hold a few minutes and start reaping the benefits. Here, a little each day goes a long way. Train it as often as possible, for just a couple of minutes, and you'll see tremendous progress.

For the first-timer, here are some pointers to help you out:

- When you step on the rope, in its middle, and extend it upwards with one hand, the length of the rope should stop at around the armpit level;
- Favor a rope made of a heavier material like plastic (rather than string);
- Work it one jump at a time. Focus on getting the timing right;
- Keep your elbows to your sides. Don't stretch your arms out;
- Look straight ahead, not at your feet;
- It's the wrists that should make the rotation, not the arms;
- Jump only when the rope is coming under you. Don't bounce 3 times in place for every one rotation.

Once you're comfortable with this basic jumping technique, you'll want to vary the tricks to work your muscles and coordination differently, and get your legs used to changing rhythms.

Amongst the many variations you can include, here are the most common:

- Double-unders (you will make 2 rotations per jump);

- Switching jumps with your feet together with jumps on one foot then the other;
- Jump repeatedly on one foot before going to the other;
- Lift your knees up as high as you can on every step;
- Jump from side to side (like a skier);
- Jump from front to back.

All those moves will teach your feet to work together seamlessly. You will gain in coordination and fluidity.

Speed Ladder Drills to Make You More Agile than a Monkey

Another nice tool to work your agility with and which works in a lot of ways like the jumping rope is the speed ladder. More often than not, you'll see football and soccer players use it rather than fighters, but that's only because the latter never learned how to implement this very handy item into their program.

In essence, a speed ladder is nothing more than a piece of plastic about 20 feet long and 20 inches wide, and which – hold your breath! – looks like a ladder when placed on the floor. Like a ladder, it's made of a series of rungs which delineate diverse areas where you'll be landing your feet while going through it. Those rungs can be adjusted to your liking to vary distances and change the difficulty.

In my opinion, it represents a great complement to the jumping rope as, though it works the same abilities (coordination, footwork, balance, control), it does so in an entirely different fashion. Now, instead of jumping up and down, you're covering distances and have to pay extra attention to stay within the limits of your squares and not touch the rungs. As a result, you'll gain in precision and responsiveness as well.

There exist lots of drills to use with a speed ladder. Here are the most effective for the warrior in training:

- **Quick steps**: the first drill everyone starts with is not only the easiest but the best in my eyes (I love to keep things simple in case you hadn't figured yet.) Standing in front of the ladder, step inside the first square with your left foot, then progress to the second with the right. Move in this manner until you've reached the end of the ladder. Obviously, you'll want to go as fast as possible while staying on the balls of your feet the whole time;
- **2 forward, 1 back**: here, both feet will enter each square. But after you've moved up 2 squares, you'll go back 1. Great for coordination;
- **Side steps**: with the ladder laid out to your right, hop into the first square laterally with your right foot. Join in with the left before moving on to the next square;
- **Left-right/Right-left**: this time, we'll still be moving sideways but with the ladder stretching in front of us. With the first square to your right, get inside with your right foot and follow with your left. Then exit the square on the other side by moving your feet to the right of the next square. And repeat.

While speed ladder drills make for a nice addition to our program, I wouldn't rely on them too much for building our footwork. Even though they work wonders for improving feet coordination, the movements available for those drills only vaguely resemble those employed when fighting. That's why they'll be mostly used as a warm-up exercise with added benefits.

Baby Steps All the Way

This is, in a certain way, the continuity of the 2 previous sections. Its application to fighting, if you will. When training your techniques or sparring, move in small increments (like you do when jumping rope or using the speed ladder); don't try and bounce from one side of the room to the other as if you had put the Seven-league boots on. Short and energetic steps; here's the winning formula we'll be covering in depth in the next chapter.

How to Improve the Speed of Your Attacks

Moving your body through space and "closing the distance" are only part of the total equation. Once you're within reach of your opponent, you still need to unload with sufficient speed so as to hit him square before he backs off. Footwork is only worth anything when met with quick hands.

Before we proceed with the techniques that will get us there, it's important to note that when training for speed, you should always push to your maximum. You won't make any gains if you take it easy or keep gas in your tank. That's why your drills should be like our HIIT and MetCons sessions from our previous program: short and intense. And that's also why you'll always want to train them first, when you're still fresh and ready to give it a hundred percent.

Boxing with the Shadows

Once you've trained your technique assiduously and got your kicks and punches pretty much rooted, you'll be ready to tackle shadowboxing. If jumping rope and doing ladder drills can help bring your coordination and agility up to par, there's no secret: to learn the right way to move during a fight, you have to fight (or pretend you're fighting)!

Shadowboxing is what it's all about, the ABC of building speed and precise motility. This is where we'll use the baby steps I alluded to above, to travel through space. Somehow, shadowboxing can be likened to a battle against one or several imaginary foes. Personally, I like to visualize shadowy forms appearing out of thin air and vanishing before my eyes.

It helps with keeping your speed up at all times and staying on high alert as you need to hit these visions before they disappear back into darkness. They'll be attacking as well, from all sides; so you'll need to dodge and counterattack with combinations of your own. You'll need to make each move count.

To ensure you come out on top, you'll have to vary your attacks and your rhythm so they can never read you like an open book. Surprise them. Duck, follow with a cross and a hook. Move back, parry, and pounce forward with a double jab-leg kick.

This technique will teach you to think on your feet. It works so well because you're not just training your moves and your brain-muscle connections with it. By visualizing opponents and going through this fictional battle, you're actually prepping yourself for a future encounter!

You see, the brain does not make much difference between real and imagined. When you're picturing something in your mind, the same neural areas will activate as if you were really experiencing it. Specific pathways will reinforce and you'll have a much easier time dealing with that very situation next time you face it.

Start with a few minutes here and there, every time you train. And build up to 5 rounds of 3 minutes. If you want, you can change the emphasis on each round by focusing, for example, on your footwork for 3 minutes, then your punches, your kicks, simple 1-2 combos, more elaborate combinations, and so on.

Mind Your Breath

This is not so much a drill as it is a piece of advice to instantly increase your quickness on all moves. When you're dancing around, throwing attacks as fast as you can, you can't reach full speed if everything about you isn't in tune with your objective.

I mean that you can't be fast in your strikes if you're slow "upstairs" or if you're breathing deeply as if shooting yourself up with the smell of donuts. Your attitude, attention as well as body functions should all be focused on having you break the sound barrier.

Be aware of your surroundings but stay on your target. Be in the present, as Zen monks would tell you. Keep your wits sharp and be ready to act or react at the drop of a hat.

Your breath should flow with your attacks, exploding with every strike. Only then will it all click.

Training Speed with a Bag

When it comes to footwork and the speed of your strikes, there's just no comparison. You have shadowboxing on one side, then you have the rest on the other. However, while you punch and kick the air, if you stay relaxed as you should, no matter how fast you'll go you'll rarely feel the burn. You will not tire out. But in a real fight, your blows will be met with resistance. You'll get parried, your hooks will crash into your opponent's guard... all of which will absorb energy and lead to fatigue.

Suddenly, you've thrown a couple of combinations and you're not that fast anymore. What happened? To be quick (and remain so throughout your bout), you need to build muscle endurance. And using a bag – or any other such item that will take your hits without protesting – is one great way to achieve that goal.

What I like to do is choose 1 technique, whether punch or kick, and go all out for 20 seconds, trying to land as many of them as possible. I'll then wait 40 seconds, to ensure my muscles have recovered enough to start again. I'll do this for 10 minutes and call it a day. This will have your limbs beg for mercy, yet the stamina gains will blow your mind.

In closing, I should mention that you can also use speedbags, resistance bands and medicine balls to improve your hand speed. But I'm trying to keep the equipment needed to a minimum as everybody doesn't have access to that type of tools. If you want to incorporate bodyweight training in your program, push-ups, pull-ups and box jumps will work especially well (just make sure to perform them explosively.)

Reflexes like a Fly's

Have you ever been driven crazy by a fly, gliding all around your face, mocking and teasing you? It would land a few inches from your hand, as if to say "c'mon, take your best shot, pal!" And you could almost hear it laugh as you would hit nothing but air. Ha ha ha!

That's what we want to accomplish here. No, not become obnoxious flying insects and end up like Jeff Goldblum after his experiment gone wrong. We want to develop the same type of reflexes as them so that when someone tries to crush us with their fist, we'll already be out of the way.

Working your reaction time is tricky as it often requires a partner and/or equipment. You need someone or something to produce the stimuli to which you'll react. Though shadowboxing will help (by imagining those attacks), it's more practical to train this with someone else. So, if you know a friend who'd like to embark on this adventure with you, convince him to start... Lend him this book and follow this journey together. It will be a much less lonely road that way.

Mitts and Pad Work

The key to developing superfast reflexes is to become so acquainted with a move that you can sense it the very moment your opponent thinks about launching it! You will recognize a slight twitch of the shoulder or a change in the position of his hips and instantly recognize what's coming. But to reach that level of anticipation, it takes time, and training.

One of the best ways to develop that faculty is by making use of mitts. Now, that means that you would need not only a partner in crime but also that you two invest in a pair of speed mitts. So, this might not be an option for you if you're training on your own. In that case, go down a few paragraphs and utilize the other techniques I'll share with you.

However, if you've managed to drag someone into this mad quest, here's how to make the best use of your mitts:

- For one, don't leave them up all the time. We're trying to improve our reaction time here; so we need a visual stimulation, some type of green light that will tell us when to go and unload. That will be you lifting up the mitts (usually, people use their voice to tell the other to go but it's better to focus on visual cues as that's what we base our reactions on in a real fight situation. Not spoken words);
- Raise a mitt for a brief second, then bring it back down. It will force your partner to strike fast or risk missing the target;
- Change rhythms. Lift the mitts several times in a row, then leave them down for a few seconds. Make it unpredictable;

- Strike with the mitts as well to have the other work both his defensive and offensive reflexes.

Sparring

Still got that partner of yours? Let's make it a little more fun and challenging! There's no secret really, to get prepared to getting punched and kicked at, nothing will ever substitute to the real thing.

Put on a pair of gloves, a mouth guard, shin protections and a cup, and get ready to scrap. Before you try and take each other's head off, let me add that, for training reflexes, it's much better to spar casually. To get used to "sensing" the attacks, you need to move slowly. If you go too fast, you won't be able to see the attacks coming and you will therefore not benefit from them.

Sparring gently will also give you the opportunity to study the way your partner moves and how each technique is thrown. Observe his shoulders, his torso and hips. Notice how they rotate, twitch and pivot as each combination is performed.

If no one can be bothered to lift their butt off their sofa to either train with you or, at the very least, give you a hand, here are some other options to exercise on your own. Yes, sometimes you can only rely on yourself... but that will only make your success the sweeter!

Mirror Shadowboxing

Find a large mirror in front of which to box. This isn't to admire your pecs or check out how cool you look when throwing strikes. Watching yourself while shadowboxing will allow you to "see" the attacks from every angle. It will allow you to understand human motion in a fighting situation; what it looks like when you're delivering a cross or a front kick, or when you're about to move to the side.

If you want to execute your blows and footwork as fast as you can when looking to improve your speed; here, I would take it down a notch to ensure, as with slow sparring, that you get enough time to analyze the movements.

With that being said, everybody doesn't move in the same way. So, training with the same partner day in day out and watching yourself shadowbox will only get you so far. You also ought to study other fighters.

Watching Others Train and Fight

We won't be too picky here. Whether it's pro boxers, kickboxers or MMA fighters, they should all do. Watch what tickles your fancy. In fact, the more diverse the competitors, the better. By observing those guys in the ring, you'll learn the cues leading to an attack, a feint or a dodge.

Don't hesitate to play some sequences in slow motion to better detect those small hints. In a way, it works like with visualization. When watching someone else fight, mirror neurons in your brain will fire as if you were yourself throwing down. They will not only help you to become more proficient at these techniques (without even needing to step a foot in the ring), they will also – as believed by scientists – get you to better understand other people's intentions as mirror neurons are at the root of the imitation process.

In other words, by watching seasoned fighters go at it, you'll have a much easier time stringing your combinations together next time it's your turn to battle!

Maize & Double End Bags

Using bags for building reflexes may not be as effective as the previous methods as they only vaguely resemble actual punches and kicks. It's for that reason that I don't recommend training with tennis balls or playing dodge ball. Improvements in those areas will seldom translate to increased fighting reflexes.

However, training with the two bags described below can still be useful, if not for injecting some diversity into your program, to train your slips and dodging technique. Moreover, you can build them on the cheap or buy them second-hand on an auction site, and they don't take too much room to install.

The first item that may benefit you is the maize bag. It's a small bag filled with beans, rice or whatever you got on hand, and which you'll hang from the ceiling at head height with a rope. Once set in motion, it will start swinging like a pendulum for minutes. It's not very quick but it can get you used to moving away from the source of danger. Step in when it backs out, step out when it comes in. Make it so that the distance between you and the bag remains identical. Mix your footwork with bounces to the side, come back at an angle with some punches of your own.

The other bag that may prove useful is the double end bag. Attached on both sides, that bag moves much faster than the maize and it will require quicker reflexes on your part to hit it and avoid getting your nose smashed when it retracts back with full force.

When you strike, you may be surprised to see it bounce back almost immediately. It will force you to stay on your toes and develop fast eyes. Throw combos at it, move around and dodge. Slowly but surely, you'll see your reaction time improve.

"Flexible, Not Break"

In the same manner that "bricks not hit back", "flexible not break" (I know, 2 Bloodsport references in less than 20 pages, I'm pushing it... Sorry, can't help it. I just love that flick!)

I'm not ashamed to admit it. When I was a kid, I was a fan of Jean-Claude Van Damme. The best part in his movies, just like Stallone's Rocky features, were the initiations where he would transform from a rigid and clumsy Joe into a true war machine. I was especially impressed with the scenes where he would get quartered on his way to the full split. I would watch and re-watch those sequences, entirely mesmerized. What it allowed him to do! All those crazy flying back kicks and well-placed punches in the private parts. 't was a thing of pure beauty!

At that time, I didn't really concern myself with efficiency over beauty yet. Attaining the same level of flexibility as JCVD quickly became one of my priorities. So, I trained and trained, to look like yet another hero of mine.

Below, I'll share with you the best techniques I learned which provided the fastest results. But before I do, let's talk about why you should train your flexibility, as you might be wondering how relevant its place is in our program if we won't be doing flashy moves anyway.

Why You Need to Train Your Flexibility

Indeed, throwing vertical kicks to the stars will NOT be part of our strategy to dispatch an enemy. But being supple isn't all about looking good and taking pics of you doing the splits between two chairs.

Improving one's flexibility is important to prevent injuries. With stretchy muscles and tendons, you get much less risk of pulling one or incurring tears. But that's not all. With good elasticity, you also get more hitting power as you don't have to fight off the resistance from your tendons, pulling down on your legs hard.

For the same reason, you'll get less tired as each kick won't feel like you're about to burst a joint. In short, you should work on your flexibility because it'll make you more durable overall. *Capisce*?

How to Do the Splits

Despite the title of this small chapter, this isn't so much about learning to do the splits as it is to make you more flexible than you are right now. Achieving this impressive figure is not compulsory to become a good fighter who can hold his own against 99% of the population. Though it's a nice goal to aim for, as long as you get enough flexibility to throw any technique without hindrance, that should more than suffice.

So, whether you want to go all the way or would rather dedicate as little time as possible to that part of your training, the principles won't change much.

For good flexibility, you'll have to work on your groin and hamstrings. And your lower back, calves and hip flexors to a lesser degree. We could go into a scientific analysis of our muscle fibers and tendons, but let's just say – for the sake of clarity – that they're like elastics. If you pull on them and keep the stretch long enough, eventually, they will loosen.

It also means that if you go at it too hard, you may risk snapping them as well! The correct technique for safe stretching will thus be to apply a light and constant pull. That's why static stretches work best. Just get into the designated position and keep it for at least 1 minute. If you can't hold that long, it means you're pulling too hard.

To ensure you're giving your muscles a good stretch, you need to cover every angle. Here are the exercises I usually go through, in order:

The Forward Bend

I often start standing with my legs spread wide in such a manner as to feel a slight stretch in their back. I then bend forward to accentuate the stretch, count to 20, and turn to the side to grab my left leg or ankle. I count once again to 20, while trying to touch my head to my knee. And I do the same with the other side. The forward bend will stretch every part of your body involved in kicking. It's a great exercise to begin your session with. To put the emphasis a little bit more on the hamstrings, calves and lower back, bring your legs closer together.

The Heel Stretch

From the forward bend, I will usually go down on one heel (as if doing a side-to-side squat) and stretch my legs in that position. By lowering yourself on one leg, you will increase the stretch at the groin level.

The Hip Flexor Stretch

Next, you will get yourself in a lunge, that is with one knee up, one knee on the ground. And you will push with your hips forward to really work those flexors.

The Butterfly Stretch

After that, I usually finish with stretches on the floor. The first of them being the butterfly. In a seated position, press the soles of your feet together, grab your feet and bring them close to your buttocks.

Lean forward to increase the tension and lower those knees as much as is comfortably possible.

The Straddle Stretch

In my eyes, this is the most effective tool to gain flexibility and the one I focus on the most. The fact that you're on the ground will allow you to keep that position more easily than when crouching or standing. It will also make it easier for you to increase the tension bit by bit.

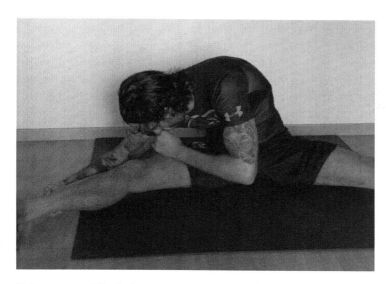

Before you straddle the legs, you may want to perform the exercise with each leg separately. To do that, simply keep one leg in the butterfly position and stretch the other in front of you. Try and grab your toes. Your aim will be to bring your head to your knee.

There are other stretching routines you can use but, if you keep working on those 5 we just detailed, you should see great results. No need for other drills. To achieve the splits, you'll have to work at it for several months. As with any skill worth your while, you can't develop it overnight.

A quick note before we jump to the next part and discover how to seriously increase our hitting power and strengthen our body: stretching is best left for the end of your workout when your muscles are loose and warm. I will usually stretch for 10 minutes as part of my cool down.

Alright, you're still with me? Good. Let's learn how to SMASH like Hulk!

PART III

Power Training & Body Strengthening: Develop a Tough Skin and Sledgehammers for Fists

*"Hit 'em hard --
don't give 'em time to react!"*

Nova

As we've seen in Part II with the E = MC² formula, speed and power are closely intertwined. To produce a lot of energy (and damage/destruction), you need a high velocity... but you also need a substantial mass behind it.

Most people's punches are weak because – their poor technique notwithstanding – they're using their meager 5lbs arms to strike. So that's how many pounds of force they're really backing their attack up with! In other words, they could have an arm as big as Arnold's in his prime that it would only have little more impact than a slap.

To make true power yours, you need to understand where it comes from, how it's generated.

How Power Is Created – Proper Technique for Maximum Damage

Compared to the common man, real fighters attack by moving like one block, like one tight ball. They don't throw their arm or leg at their adversary as if it was some foreign limb they were trying to get rid of; they're putting their whole body into it.

They learned to recruit every major muscle with each strike so that it's not 5lbs but close to 100% of their mass that gets accelerated and transformed into pure energy! As if one giant wall of bricks was rushing towards their enemy to crush them!

The Secret

To discover the secret to power, you ought to first grasp the body mechanics that will allow you to involve your entire bodyweight in each blow.

As we've been hinting from the start of this book, much of our attacks will start from the hips. You know why? Because that's the link between your lower and upper body; that's the hinge that will transfer the energy from your legs to your punches (or from your torso to your kicks.) Indeed, it is with the rotation it permits that the energy will flow through our body all the way to the point of impact. We will rotate, pivot on the balls of our feet and, provided we use correct technique, each body part will add its own weight to the equation. BAM! Next thing you know, each of your strikes will hurt like a mack truck!

It's for that very reason that pushing weights and focusing on building huge triceps in order to hit harder doesn't help much. At the risk of repeating myself, you're not punching with the muscles of your arms. You're really punching with your entire body.

I know that it's easier said than done, that it sounds like a piece of cake but that it can take a while to finally "get it". With using your hips, it's like every other movement you'll learn here. You need to drill it until it becomes second nature. At first, it will feel strange and you'll have trouble giving that torque at the right moment to shift your weight as you should. But as you keep practicing, the brain-muscle connections getting reinforced, you will slowly get better until the lightbulb eventually turns on. When it does, you should be able to apply that technique to every punch and kick in your arsenal.

The Technique

OK, so now you know you'll have to rotate your body to generate that power. But that's not it. You could still be making mistakes in your form that could cost you a lot if not all of that power.

When launching an attack, here are a few key points to watch out for:

First of all, pay attention to your center of gravity. When throwing a punch, most people move their torso too much forward and shift their weight from their rear leg to that in the front as if it was that shifting from one foot to the other that produced the power.

You're not heaving your body at the enemy, my friend, unless you've decided to take him out WWE style! When you go in such a manner, from back to front, your torso gets out of line and you lose both power and balance as your center of gravity gets out from "under" you. You need to keep your weight spread equally between both legs when throwing your punch. To manage an effective rotation, you need both legs solidly anchored (one pushing, the other pulling on the ground.) It also means that you should keep your knees flexed to have your center closer to the ground.

The same precepts apply to your kicks. Stay low with your body aligned to generate as much torque as possible and get a better balance.

Another thing you want to avoid is to hit too fast. I know what you're thinking, we've been spending a lot of time talking about how to be as quick as possible and now I'm telling you to slow down? What the heck is wrong with me? Don't be too harsh on me, my friend. I cry easily. *Starts sobbing.*

Jokes aside, I'm not asking you to drop the pace per say. The problem many people encounter when striking as fast as they can is that they end up whipping their moves. They throw them and bring their arm or leg back before their hips had a chance to work their magic. Ultimately, they only manage to get a fraction of their weight behind their technique.

In short, it always comes down to the same thing: correct form. You should only go as fast as you can while maintaining perfect technique and being able to put your torque into it.

One last mistake I often see is when people try to go right for the kill. Instead of building their combinations, they rush for the one shot knock-out with a right bomb or a high kick. Not setting up your big attack will make it that much more telegraphed. Your opponent will have no problem seeing it coming and counterattacking with a haymaker of his own. Leading your combo with a jab, for example, is also important for power because it puts your body in the perfect position to rotate and really use those hips.

The Recap

All that talk about hips and torque may still sound alien to you. That's why I'll try to give you an overview of how the energy is created in every part of your body and how it travels all the way to the point of impact.

In the case of a punch:

- Your knees bend;
- Your feet pivot in the direction of the attack;
- Your hips rotate;

- Your torso follows the movement and spins while remaining in line with your hips;
- You punch and see your attack speed up with all the built-up energy from the lower body;
- Your fist lands and transmits all that power to the lucky recipient;
- You return to your stance.

For a kick, the first few steps remain identical. You'll just lift your foot before you pivot, so that your leg moves (and hits) with your entire body.

Exercises for Punching Harder

As with speed, before you train your power, you'll need to have mastered the technical side first. Learning to use your hips and putting all your weight behind your punches and kicks will account for 80% of your success.

To get the last 20%, here are a few drills you can incorporate in your training to maximize your efficiency.

Bag and Pad Work

If practice makes perfect, you can't develop real power by merely shadowboxing and swinging at the air. While it's good for building speed, to become a true knock-out artist you need to familiarize yourself with the feeling of your fists crashing into something else. This is the only way to acquire the right touch for hitting hard.

Using a bag (and/or a pad) represents an essential part of it. It will provide a target that's firm enough to absorb the energy from your blows but not to the point of causing injury. You will focus on your torque on every strike, trying to punch or kick through that bag.

After each hit, wait for the bag to come back before you go at it again. Try and stop it dead in its tracks.

Learn Your Optimal Range

If you remember what we said when we were talking about "rolling with the punches", attacks are at their strongest when they land at about 75-80% of their full extension. That's why we need to become true masters of distances. How can you hit your adversary at the right moment if you can't judge how far your fist still has to travel before it lands?

To train your eye, bag work helps of course. But I like to take it a step further to make sure I really know my distances to the millimeter. Standing in front of a bag (or a wall, if you want to play it dangerously), throw jabs and crosses, and stop your attacks right before they make contact.

Obviously, you'll want to start slow to get a feel for it and avoid tearing your knuckles to shreds. Once you get the hang of it, slowly pick up the pace. At this point, you should still be standing still. Only introduce moving around, in and out, when you can go at full speed and not even scratch the wall.

Then, you can let loose with different combinations and begin adding kicks to the drills.

Learn the Perfect Timing

The problem is that we'll never have to fight a wall (unless you've been locked away by a villain or took too much drugs and start seeing "things".) Your opponent will not wait for you to get your distances right so you can land your victory punch at precisely 80% of its extension. He will be moving around!

Which means that if you got your range under control, you still need to be able to anticipate the movements of your opponent to catch him at the right time.

For starters, you want to observe how he moves to try and find his particular rhythm. Most people know so little about fighting that they don't bother changing their pace; they'll always move uniformly, that is until they become too gassed to move at all.

The best moment to strike is when your opponent moves towards you. There's no easier way to achieve a KO. In a sense, this would be the opposite of rolling with the punches as your adversary steps right into yours and gets his chin a warm welcome.

You'll also want to be on the lookout for telltale signs like the loading of a punch or backing away a few inches to throw a kick. Inexperienced fighters will telegraph their attacks, which makes reading their mind and stepping in with a jab of your own that much easier. A jab that you'll follow with a straight, left hook combination.

Another way to dominate the battle is to corner the other guy and prevent him from moving at all. Be the aggressor; push him back until he has nowhere else to go. His back against the wall, he'll be that much easier to strike.

Compound Movements

Like I said, building huge arms will not be worth your time as your delts, biceps and triceps only have but a minor role to play in power generation. However, training compound movements that target your body's biggest muscle chains may help a little more. With stronger legs and back muscles, you'll be able to induce a more powerful torque that will translate into faster acceleration and more energy in the end.

So, if you want to add strength training to your regimen, I would recommend focusing on squats, deadlifts and clean & presses (for more information on those, report back to volume 01: strength & conditioning.)

Body Strengthening: Build Your Natural Armor

Fighting isn't all about inflicting damage, though. If you can't take a punch or deliver one and not break your fingers in the process, you're not that much better off.

When it comes to hardening your body, there will be 2 sides to the training. The first one will aim to make you tougher and more resilient. The second will seek to make your primary weapons (fists and shins) as solid as steel.

How to Toughen Up

I'm not going to lie, getting punched in the face isn't the most pleasurable thing ever but you can learn to take a hit and still smile about it. In the end, it's all about preparation and managing to keep your cool.

Bend like a Reed in the Wind

Staying relaxed under enemy fire is paramount, not only because it makes your moves faster and more powerful, but also because it allows you to take punishment more efficiently. Once again, it goes back to our precept of "rolling with the punches"... If you're stiff, you're opposing a counter force to any incoming projectile; therefore, you'll take the shots at full power. On the other hand, if you leave your body flexible, you'll be able to go with the flow and absorb some of that power. That makes sense, doesn't it?

By retaining your composure, you will also keep a better track of your opponent's movements. When you stress out and start panicking, you lose sight of your adversary's rhythm and can't see the obvious signs preceding an attack anymore. And like we said earlier, those are the strikes that hurt the worst. Those that you feel more than you see, and that make you taste defeat.

When you stay sharp, even if you get punched or kicked at, you can still brace for the impact when you see the missile coming at full speed towards your stomach. Try to do that with your eyes closed!

But if getting hit isn't so much a question of "if" as of "when", it also means that we need to get our body in proper condition. You can improve your ability to take a shot by preparing physically. The 2 main areas that require our attention are: the neck and the abdominals. Why? Because a stronger neck offers more protection for those times when you get clocked by a hard shot. It will act as a cushion, or a brake, and avoid the snapping back of your head. Your chances of staying on your feet will improve dramatically, and you'll be less likely to suffer a concussion.

As for the abs, with proper groundwork, they'll become like a shield that keeps your vital organs safe and that prevents you from ending up like a darn fish out of water, gasping for air.

Training the Neck

The most common exercise to work your neck is to use a harness with a few pounds attached to it and – leaning forward – to bring your head back and forth by contracting your muscles. Sets of 10 repetitions are good. However, it implies that you have a harness to begin with. If that's not the case, you can substitute that with a towel, your hands or any other item that will allow you to exert a pressure on the back of your head.

Just remember to train using every axis of rotation. You want to develop a strong neck overall so that wherever you get punched from, no matter the angle, you'll get protected.

Two other exercises I like to train do not require any equipment. The first is the headstand, where you will use your head in support of your hands to lift your body up in the air. The second is the neck bridge where you can increase the difficulty by taking your hands completely off the floor.

Training the Abs

You admire Bruce Lee and want to take a page out of his book? Do like the Little Dragon and train with a medicine ball. Lie on the floor and have someone drop one from a height. This can help you learn to stay relaxed until that very second where the shockwave reaches your guts and you need to tighten your abs to absorb it.

That's one way to get used to receiving body shots. Another is to have someone wear boxing gloves and start pampering your ribs with hooks and straights. No need to go all out and injure yourself here; small, frequent blows go a long way.

Those are nice for sure but, personally, I like to focus my abs training on developing strength. A strong core will benefit you on so many different levels... It will not only make you more powerful and explosive, it will improve your posture and back health. To get the best results, forget about crunches and sit-ups. The 2 exercises to put your efforts into are: the L-sit and the toes-2-bar.

As their names suggest, for the first one you will be sitting down with your legs completely off the floor (and parallel to it), in such a way as to make an L shape with your torso.

As for toes-2-bar, hanging from a bar, lift your feet up until your toes come in contact with the bar.

Other useful exercises to consider include Russian twists and windshield swipes, both of which target the obliques which are important for liver protection.

3 sets of 6-10 repetitions is what I recommend per exercise. For the L-sit, try and keep the position for 10 good seconds.

In addition to the neck & abs, some people choose to condition their legs as well for low kicks defense. But that's not really needed in my opinion. It takes years to get used to receiving kicks to the thighs, and we don't have that much time. Anyway, opponents you'll meet in the streets will seldom throw such kicks, even less an effective one. All you need to know is how to check. That's it.

What should sit atop of your list, though, is to learn how to be a better fighter overall. When you've mastered every combination, you'll become that much better at defending against them. It's like with chess: when you get to the point that you can recognize an opening the very moment someone moves a piece, you'll get such an unfair advantage that no one will be able to surprise you anymore.

Sharpen Your Tools of Destruction

If I advise you to always carry of pair of light leather gloves in your pocket to offer some type of protection to your delicate hands in case you need to crack a skull or two, you won't always have the time to put them on. So, you must ensure you've made them hard enough to withstand any shock and not yield.

I can't tell you how much it blows to break a hand and find yourself unable to punch. And you can imagine, I'm sure, your chances of getting out of there alive if it happened to your shins! Hardening one's means of offense should be part of any fighter's program.

How Strengthening Works

First, a quick word on your bones, to help you understand how we'll go about strengthening them.

You may think that bones are unlike other parts of your body such as your hair or your skin which are constantly evolving as new cells are produced and old cells get discarded. You may think that they're like the pillars of a home; once set, they won't move or change that much. The truth is that bones are exactly the same! Made up of collagen, calcium and phosphate, they're always fluctuating between creation and destruction.

Our goal with thus be to promote bone growth so that the plus side of the equation prevails over the minus, and your bones get denser and harder. To do that, it works just like with muscle building: by creating small traumas that, when repaired with extra calcium deposits, will leave the "injured" area slightly stronger than before.

Stone-Hard Fists

To "damage" our hands and make them harder, we can have recourse to different techniques. Keep in mind that hands represent one of the body's most complex and fragile parts. When training or using them to defend yourself, always make sure you strike with perfect technique. Don't let your punches land with your fist not properly closed or right on one finger. You want to strike with your knuckles and watch those wrists.

The first tool at our disposal to strengthen those knuckles, but also the skin that covers them, is our good old punching bag. If you'll probably wear boxing gloves as you start training, you'll want to move to smaller gloves and continue reducing the protection until you're using but your bare hands. This will work wonders to build calluses on your knuckles.

If a punching bag isn't part of your options, you can get a makiwara board which is an ancient Karate piece of equipment which serves the same purpose. You can build one easily with dry straw that you'll bundle together with pieces of string. Old telephone books can do as well.

A softer approach to punching the bag until your hands bleed is to dig your fists into a basket containing rice or sand. The repeated friction of the grains against your skin will quickly bolster the generation of new cells.

Once you've built some padding courtesy of your dead cells, you can choose to add fist push-ups to the mix to train your strength at the same time. When performing those, pay attention to your elbows and the position of your hands. For the best results, keep your elbows glued to your sides and your fists closed with their palms facing your body. For starters, execute your sets on a carpet or other such soft surfaces. And as you gain resistance, move on to harder grounds like wood and concrete. Eventually, you'll be able to do your push-ups on gravel.

Strong fists aren't all about the knuckles though. If you decide to use push-ups in your training regimen, you may also want to add finger push-ups. By pressing your bodyweight up and down on the tip of your fingers, you will build up their strength and reinforce their bones and joints.

Shins like a Thai's

If you check on the Internet how to condition your legs for fighting, you'll see all sorts of crazy stuff advertised like kicking banana trees, rolling empty glass bottles on your shins or hitting them hard with a bamboo stick to kill the nerves.

Although we all dream in secret of cracking a trunk in two like JCVD (not him again!) in the Kickboxer movie, those insane feats are best left to Muay thai experts who've been training their shins since they were barely able to walk. With time, their legs have become so desensitized and their bones so dense that it's almost as if they were kicking with thick soccer shin guards on.

We, mere mortals, won't need to resort to such extremes to reach our goals of becoming supermen of the fighting game. On the contrary, performing any of the aforementioned techniques would be the quickest ticket to injury and getting sidelined for weeks if not months. Moreover, this ain't a guide to teach you how to beat 99% of people in 100 months but in 100 days!

So, how hard is too hard? What level of "pain" should we aim for to properly condition those darn bones? The rule is to always pick a target that's softer than your shins. Going the other way around would only put them at risk.

Just like your fists, the best method to condition your shins is no secret: use a heavy bag. Kicking a bag over and over again will get your body used to the feeling until it becomes so natural that the brain stops caring and sending any pain signal. As you progress, change the filling inside the bag to make it heavier and harder. Pieces of cloth and leather can lead to sand, and so on.

Sparring, if you have a partner, will also greatly help. Nothing can better prepare you for that oh so special shin-to-shin contact. Go lightly and wear protections. Remember that it will take time to desensitize those legs. As in the famous fable, slow and steady is what will bring you to success here. Not sado-masochistic practices out of a bad ninja flick.

Do's and Don'ts of Striking

Knowing where to hit your opponent is almost as important as prepping your limbs to do it. Land a punch to the wrong area and, no matter how tough your knuckles have become, you're not going to like it one bit! Touch the right spot, on the other hand, and it's the guy facing you who'll be wincing in pain.

Here are the body parts you want to avoid if you care about your fists and shins' integrity:

- When you punch someone's face, watch out for the top of the head, right above the forehead. It's so thick and strong that it can smash your bones to pieces;
- When kicking the body with a roundhouse, pay attention not to get your shin into the opponent's elbow. I promise that you'll think twice about throwing that kick again after that;

- When kicking the legs, if hitting the knee when it's extended is good practice as it can help diminish your adversary's mobility, striking its tip when it's flexed is bad, really bad news for you. It can end up breaking your leg.

Now, onto the good stuff! The best parts to target to make your enemy quit and still keep the fight "honorable" (for dirty fighting, I'll see you back in Part V):

- **The solar plexus**: when you hear one punch KO, you probably think about a good right cross to the chin. However, aiming for the spot right below the sternum can accomplish the same goal. Punch someone there and he'll feel like you've ripped his lungs out of his chest. Not only because he won't be able to breathe anymore, but also because of the excruciating pain he'll feel throughout his thorax;
- **The liver**: another good spot most people overlook is the liver. Yet, this organ is amongst the most important in the human body, responsible for more functions and processes we could possibly list in this book. When it's struck, along with the vagus nerve that's connected to it, the body will go into shock. The effects will be reminiscent of a blow to the solar plexus but even a little more acute; it will bend you in two and have you want to curl up in a ball and die. The nerve is located on the right side of the body, above the waist. It is vulnerable to uppercuts, hooks and middle kicks to the ribcage. By aiming for it, with a little luck, you might even break a rib or two;
- **The nose**: no other body part comes as soft and sweet as the cartilage of the nose. The effects of a nose hit are immediate. Sharp pain, blurred vision as your eyes tear up... On top of this, noses are known to break like glass, causing all sorts of nice perks like disrupted breathing or eyes getting swollen if not closed shut. Noses are particularly susceptible to hooks;
- **The "button"**: the holy grail of every fighter, the aim of so many warriors trying to end it all with one homerun punch, the chin is not that painful compared to the body when it's struck. But, boy, does it get the job done! If it's called the button, it's simply because there's no other way to turn somebody's lights off as easily as with a push of that switch. To get the KO, though, you need a quick and violent head turn. If your blow lands too far up the jaw, the head movement will be minimal and you won't bring the tower down;
- **The thigh**: for the lower body, one of your prime targets will be the first third of the outer legs, right above the knees. This part is highly innervated and will send electric shocks throughout the adversary's body as you kick him there. Limping usually ensues.

It's all nice and well to know the theory and to practice for a possible showdown. But what if you get paralyzed once you're dealing with the real thing? What if, stricken with fear, you get overwhelmed by your emotions and can't use any of those techniques you've learned?

If training your body to fight is crucial, you also need to train your mind to cope with the stress of the situation. This will NOT be like your sparring sessions where you can rest in between rounds or make a hand signal to stop for a sec if you get hurt by a blow or need to readjust your cup. You must be ready in a snap and keep enough cool to react intelligently. Introducing the psychology of fighting...

PART IV

The Psychology of Fighting:
Tame the Fear and Get the Upper Hand

*"Fear isn't necessarily a bad thing.
It tells you what's important to you.
Life. Security. Family.
But if you let your actions become
all about the fear itself, it's so easy to
destroy what that fear is urging you
to protect."*

Miriam Sharpe (Civil War)

Getting involved in a fight is one of the most stressful events you'll ever encounter in your life, no doubt about it. What makes it so hard to deal with is that, for one, it happens suddenly, meaning you won't get time to prepare for it. But more worrying yet, your brain will realize you're now facing a serious risk of bodily harm, so it will start unloading all kinds of chemicals in your blood which are supposed to help but which can (and will) rapidly play against you.

Why Do We "Lose It"?

The Fight or Flight Response

We've all heard of the fight or flight response which states that, when we find ourselves in danger, our body will undergo a sudden and dramatic physiological upheaval to get ready to either protect itself with everything it got (to the death if need be) or get the hell out of Dodge ASAP!

This is a built-in reaction we all possess and which is older than our very species. We inherited it from our ancestors who saw their lives saved thanks to it. Those who had that peculiar trait were more likely to survive an encounter with a predator than those who were happy to just stand there and watch whether that saber-toothed tiger that was rushing towards them was friend or foe. Thus, the incidence of their genes increased in the pool.

It's become an instinct, an uncontrollable reflex that can quickly overwhelm us. That's what made it so powerful back then; the fact that it's instantaneous. If people had had to think before they took act, they would have long been devoured.

The problem is that it also interferes with your ability to think and perform. Indeed, the part of the brain that takes over when danger comes a-knocking (what we call the reptilian brain) is the most archaic and primal of them all, and when it switches on, it also shuts down the more "advanced" cerebral areas like the neocortex which are responsible for higher thinking processes and everything related to the language skills.

In this case, more than 30 hormones get released, from epinephrine and norepinephrine to dopamine, testosterone and cortisol. That huge dump may have for aim to prepare yourself for combat, but the improved blood flow and muscle tension you get on one hand may not be worth the plethora of undesirable reactions that come along with them.

To give you an overview of what happens the second your nervous system turns on the fight or flight switch, here are the most notable effects:

- An increased heartbeat to the point of feeling it pulse throughout your body;
- A shaking of the muscles, especially the legs that may feel like jelly;
- Dizziness, nausea;
- A sense of panic as you feel all of the above come crashing down on you without warning;
- A sudden release of your bladder and bowels. That's why some people end up with dark stains on their pants, seconds into a fight;

- A complete alteration of your perceptions, from time dilation to hear loss and tunnel vision. Your sense of reality will be turned on its head. You'll become blind to your surroundings (which is bad news if another enemy comes at you from the sides) and unable to think straight.

You'll see that, although it means well with this chemical avalanche, the body is really shooting itself in the foot. The fight or flight response does make us faster and stronger, but also dumber than a rock! If we are to regain control and be able to get the upper hand no matter the adversity, those are the symptoms we'll need to alleviate.

The Mechanisms of Fear

So far, we've described what happens to us on a physiological level when thrown into a threatening situation. But even if the fight or flight response plays a huge role in how we feel – as the symptoms we experience feed on themselves to have us panic more and more to the point of passing out –, it does not dictate how we ultimately react.

How to explain that some of us freeze in the face of danger and find themselves unable to do anything if sit there and get picked apart by an assailant. And others behave as if they had just received a big shot of grade "A" pure Colombian?

Are we all equal against fear? Is it only a reaction to these chemicals we just talked about or is there a psychological part to it, something we could get a hold of? Understanding the mechanisms of fear will help us better prepare ourselves by showing us the true face of our enemy.

It's All in Our Head

Fear begins in the head, both literally and figuratively. On the "physical" plane, scientists have discovered that our fears originated from the amygdala, a small almond-shaped group of nuclei in the brain which acts as the body's alarm bell. They've found that people who had sustained lesions to their amygdala had become devoid of all fears. They had become reckless daredevils who wouldn't be fazed even if confronted by an angry Leonidas and his 300.

Before you put this book down and go fetch a knitting needle to attempt a partial lobotomy, thinking how cool that would be to erase that feeling from your life once and for all, let's reiterate something: fear, no matter how much it sucks, serves an important purpose. That's to protect us from danger. Our goal will be to tame it. Not eradicate it.

Fear can also be said to be "all in the head" because once the adrenalin and its pals are flowing through our veins and making our heart beat at triple its normal rate, then the rationalizing begins with a high possibility of aggravating the situation.

That's the worst about fear, when we let it take the reins and reduce us to slavery. That's where the difference is usually made between people who become victims and those who come out victorious.

A Question of Habit

If that mind chatter (that's set off with the coming palpitations and feeling of impending doom) is what causes us to get paralyzed, it's often brought about by the foreignness of the circumstances. We, as humans, are scared of what we don't know. We're creatures of habit who seldom like surprises, no matter how much we'd like to think otherwise. Take us out of our comfort zone and we'll be like kiddies without their mommies. On the verge of crying...

Yes, fear of the unknown is a powerful force. That's what makes us hate other human beings we don't even know, just because they're a different kind of shade, religion or sexual orientation. They're not like us, therefore they scare us. Violent encounters work the same way. They contrast so much with our usual routine that, when they occur, they leave us feeling helpless.

Feeling Out of Control
I wouldn't dare to call you a control freak (and if I did, what would you do about it anyway, eh? You want a piece of me?!) but a lot of people never learned to let go. They think they ought to remain in control, whether of themselves or the situation, no matter what.

They might be afraid of what others may think of them, of appearing foolish. Or of what could happen to them if they didn't hold all the cards anymore. So, when they find themselves out of their element, they freak out. They become hysterical, totally unable to take a step back and deal with the situation.

How to Take Control and Prevail
Looks like we've got a lot of work ahead of us, my man. Unless you didn't listen to me and did use that knitting needle after all, you're probably hindered by one or several of the fear mechanisms we just went through.

Let me reassure you; that doesn't make you a coward or a wimp. As Nelson Mandela put it: *courage is not the absence of fear, but the triumph over it. The brave man is not he who does not feel afraid, but he who conquers that fear.* We all experience dread. What we need to learn is to make it our friend so it doesn't end up crushing us.

Once Again, Practice Makes Perfect
Training extensively is not only good for bettering our movements and strikes, it can help us getting used to facing physical confrontations. If it's the fear of the unknown that cripples us, by making it a regular component of our daily life, to the point of getting intimate with it, we can get desensitized to its most deleterious effects.

Unfortunately, sparring with your best bud will not help much. Why? Because it'll be too casual; there will be no heart beating out of your chest, no shaking of the knees or urgency to throw up. You need to put yourself in the same conditions (or as close to them as possible) for your efforts to bear any fruits.

Now, I'm not suggesting you go to the nearest bar and pick a fight with the meanest, baddest looking SOB in there. There are safer ways to go about it. The best alternative that I know of is to start competing or, at the very least, join a competitive kickboxing/Muay thai/MMA club where you'll be able to spar with all types of imposing fighters who won't spare you.

The mere fact of waiting in the locker room to have your name called for your bout will teach you more about how to handle your jitters than years of training with the same people ever could. Getting in a real fight, with or without a referee, will give you a crash course in fear management. It will give you enough time (sometimes hours, when you're one of the last suckers on the card) to stay on it, analyze your feelings and make peace with them.

In short, standing up to our fear is the best way to tame it. But we need to go gradually to build our assurance. You don't get over a fear of spiders by locking yourself in a box filled with recluses and tarantulas; you first look at pictures of them, then you watch them from a distance. When you finally touch one, it'll be a small and inoffensive one.

In the same spirit, start with some light sparring to get you comfortable with the idea of attacking and getting punched at. Build from there; slowly increase the pace and the power. And finally, when you feel ready, sign up for a local tournament. That's how you'll become a (super)man, my son.

Stay Zen

Zen monks have much to teach us on keeping things in perspective and not letting our emotions get the best of us. Through decades of practice, they've honed their consciousness to such a degree they can remain calm, even when stepping on burning coals.

We don't have years to assign to disciplining our minds to such an extent, I know, but that doesn't mean we can't benefit from some of their meditation techniques. The most valuable aspect of meditation, more so than the taking our mind off the fear itself, is the breathing pattern it instills.

Usually, what sinks our ship isn't the pounding heart, the tunnel vision or any of those signs; what gets things spiral out of control is a lack of proper breathing. As they say in Yoga, breath is life. So when fear strikes and our breathing becomes shallow, what do you think happens next?

We start to hyperventilate. And as we keep over oxygenating ourselves, inhaling air like an asthmatic after a 300-yard dash, we feel our head grow light and dizzy. Chest pains ensue, with a tingling of the extremities, all of which do nothing to reassure the scared child we've turned into. So we take even more oxygen in until eventually our body shuts down.

The problem most people experience comes from their using their chest to breathe. By learning to rely on your belly instead, you can stop the vicious circle and protect yourself against its most debilitating consequences.

Belly or diaphragmatic breathing not only offers a soothing effect by providing a deeper and more efficient way of aerating ourselves, it counteracts the fight or flight response by preventing any hyperventilation. As we take our air lower in the abdomen, we become able to slow our breathing down.

To train this basic but highly effective technique, put one hand on your stomach, inhale with your nose while counting to 5. Feel your belly expand as you do. Once you've reached your count, start exhaling with the mouth for another 5 seconds. Rinse and repeat. The more you'll do it, the better you'll become at using it to calm you down.

Use the Power of Your Mind

So far, in both books, we've been talking a lot about physical power and how to develop it. But it's nothing compared to the power of the mind. They say we only use about 10% of our brain capacity. I don't know how much truth that statement holds but what's certain is that we don't use or nurture it as well as we should!

We often let our mind run like a wild horse, not putting any stop to our flow of thoughts, even when the latter are negative and bitter, and then we seem surprised when it turns against us any chance it gets. Our mind can help us achieve wonderful things. Or have us hit rock bottom. That's where the craziest ideas are born, where dreams are set in motion to later become a reality. That's also where we convince ourselves everyone is out there to get and hurt us. It's the ultimate decision maker, the entity that holds our fate in its hands. But I digress...

As far as managing our fear is concerned, one of the tricks at our disposal is, once again, visualization. We already used it to see our movements in our mind's eye and get better at them; however, the usefulness of this tool extends to all areas. Just picture yourself in a dire situation from which you'll come out on top.

Close your eyes and watch yourself walking down the street at night. Another guy, tall and massive, is coming the other way. When you two cross paths, he shoulders you. Moment of surprise, you stop dead in your tracks. Was it an accident, was it intentional? The other guy is already in your face. He says: "you've got a problem, f*****?" All of a sudden, your heart starts racing. That guy is clearly looking for trouble. You try to apologize: "my bad." But he steps forward, pushes you in the chest. You can feel the adrenalin pumping through your veins, your breathing threatening to get out of control. So you make a conscious effort to bring your breathing to your belly. You inhale slowly and focus your attention on that guy's movements. You see him bring his right arm back. He's going to throw a haymaker. Without a moment's hesitation, you smash a quick jab in his nose. Muffled sound as his head tilts backwards and he loses his balance. You leave him no time to regroup; you follow with a cross of your own and a left hook to the jaw. The other guy falls on the ground flabbergasted, not knowing what hit him. He won't be up for a couple of minutes, so you resume walking. Next time, he'll think twice before picking a fight with the wrong guy.

Yes, going through such scenarios where you kick some serious butt can serve to desensitize you to some degree by getting you used to that type of incident and emotions. As you play that movie over and over again, changing the setting, the circumstances and the attacker to vary your flexibility, your confidence will grow.

The real confidence builder, though, is to train diligently. When you'll have mastered your offense and defense, your boldness will soar. Most of the time, we get panicked because we're not certain we can defend ourselves properly. We doubt, and it's that disbelief in our abilities that gets us worried.

Another way to use your mind to prevail is to think positively. This may sound like new age BS to some of you but learning to see the silver lining in every challenge may help you overcome your fears. Negative thoughts, the mind chatter I was talking about previously, is a real plague. Not only when dealing with a foe; it can mess up your entire life. When you bash yourself constantly and end up convincing yourself you're good for nothing, it becomes a self-fulfilling prophecy.

In the end, it's about learning all you can about yourself. That's what meditation can help you achieve. What training may bring you, by pushing you past your limits. And after a while, when you'll have reflected on your existence and what makes you tick, you may discover what truly lies behind your fears. For now, you might think that it's the pain you dread or the possibility of losing control. But if you continue to dig deeper and to ask yourself the right questions, you'll realize that any fear, be it of bugs, heights or fights, refers back to the same common denominator: death.

Since that moment our species became aware of its own mortality, we've been trying by all means – physical, spiritual and magical – if not to escape it at least to postpone it as much as we could. For millennia, we've been searching for the fountain of youth and the best ways to remain "whole" until our last breath.

It's only when you'll have come to that conclusion, that it's death that holds you back, that you'll be able to free yourself from its grip and from your fears. We live on borrowed time. Death, no matter how much we try to push it back, is inevitable. We're all going to die someday. So, we need to make the most of what little time we have left. Worry is only going to waste those precious moments. Most of the time, anyway, fear is unjustified. How many times has your life really been in danger? And still, you let fear take control. You're not to blame; it's only natural; that's how we're wired. But we can fight it. And if we truly end up having to save our skin, would you want your last moments to be those of a chicken or those of a ferocious warrior? Don't let death take your soul without a fight. Grin at it and show it what you're really made of!

OK, enough with the psychobabble. Let's see how to make you an even bigger threat with our advanced fighting techniques.

PART V

Advanced Fighting Techniques: Anything Goes

"Now comes the part that really hurts."

Moon Knight

Knowing how to use your fists and shins is a good start but it won't always ensure victory. What if your opponent gets a hold of you? What if he grabs you and you're now too close to hit him? You could also find yourself cornered, with nowhere to go and 2 or 3 people coming at you. Then, what?

So far you've learned a lot on how to attack and defend yourself, but your game still shows some holes that need patching. In order to get out of any situation, even the bleakest, you ought to master the other weapons in your arsenal but also to make your surroundings work for you.

Close Range Weapons

If your strikes get worthless as your adversary backs away and you catch him near full extension, the opposite also stands true. When you don't have enough room to generate power for your punches and kicks, they'll feel like mosquito bites to him. We need to shorten our hitting range, and we do that by bending the arms and the legs and using that sweet hard bone in the middle as our pain dealer. With knees and elbows, we'll take our skills up another notch as they don't come as brutal and effective as those two.

But before we tackle the subject and see how to best use and train them, let's talk about another controversial weapon that could come in handy when you're so close to your target you can feel his stinking breath: the head.

Pros & Cons of Using the Headbutt

Your big head might not only serve to ponder the mysteries of the known universe and look pretty in front of the ladies, it can also be used as a blunt weapon to surprise the enemy. Its active range is very narrow, but when you're just at the perfect distance, it can prove to be a devastating tool that can turn things around in a snap.

Utilizing the headbutt is not without risks, though. The big cons against it all pertain to quality of execution. Before you attempt to throw any blow with your head, you need to make sure you've got the form nailed down perfect. The slightest mistake here, more than with any other technique, may lead to serious injury. If you strike at the wrong angle, you could break your nose or get KO'ed. You could also lose a tooth or two from the shock, if you don't keep your jaws tightly shut. And to make matters worse, you can't really practice the move while sparring because it's hard to go light and not hurt the other with it.

But if you can do it right, that is by: tilting your head forward a few degrees and striking with the thickest, least vulnerable part of your skull (the upper portion of your forehead), as though you were sneezing, then you'll find that headbutts are second to none when it comes to inflicting damage.

It also implies you aim at the right spot. Don't go heabutting the other bloke on his forehead as if you were two rams trying to duke it out. Don't go for the jaw either in an attempt to knock him out; you might end up with teeth lodged in your skull.

To soften the opponent up and take a major advantage, you'll want to direct your attack at his nose. You won't feel a thing as your head collides with the cartilage, but I can assure you that he will! Another alternative is to zero in on the eye socket. It doesn't take much to cut it open and, once you do, you'll see blood pouring down his face as if you had struck oil.

That might be enough to scare him (the sight of blood can make even the toughest guys panic.) And if not, it will still work in our favor as his vision gets blurred from all that blood flowing down in his eyes.

In brief, you'll probably never have the opportunity to use the headbutt much because of the range restrictions but, if the circumstances allow, go for it as this could be the only blow you throw at all!

Meet E & K, Your Two New Best Friends

When it comes to striking methods, I often take my cues from Muay thai as, even if it's not perfect in every aspect, it's still amongst the most effective fighting sports out there. One of the reasons why is through its extensive use of knees and elbows. Although they're present in other disciplines and martial arts, those two types of attacks are often relegated to a kata or a particular instance. They're not part of the regular routine, so people never learn how to use them properly. Good for us as they're missing on the best close quarters instruments!

In Thai boxing, there are around 15 different elbow and knee strikes but, once again, we'll ditch the crazy stuff like the double elbows and stick to the basics. Remember, KISS, baby!

To say that elbows are effective in the clinch would be an understatement. If you thought headbutts were efficient at causing big gashes, wait until you see elbows in action! But working as your body's razor is not its only value; it can produce extreme power in a very short distance and induce concussions as well. Hit with the tip of the elbow to graze and open your opponent's skin. Move a little further up the forearm for maximum concussive power.

In my eyes, the 2 techniques worth learning are:

- **The lateral elbow**: the technique here is similar to a hook. With the arm bent, rotate with your hips and strike horizontally;
- **The downward elbow**: this one is best used to hit the rear head when scrambling or to attack the back when your adversary is trying to grab your legs and leaves his neck and kidneys exposed. Your elbow will travel vertically and make contact with its meatier part, right above the tip where the triceps begins.

Knees are a little more versatile in that they can inflict damage to almost any part of the body. You can target the solar plexus or the liver when facing your enemy, or you can choose to weaken his legs with nasty shots to the thighs. The best area to shoot for will, of course, be the face. When you smash your knee there, you won't have to worry about what you hit. You won't feel a thing whereas the other party will find itself in a world of pain.

To knee someone, grab him by the neck and pull his head down towards your knee. Thrust your hips forward as you arch your back and shoot your knee upwards. Bruises guaranteed!

If you're taller than the average, you could also use those knees as you would kicks to the face and send them directly to your opponent's jaw.

When it comes to training, both elbows and knees do not differ from other strikes. They're best drilled on the heavy bag for power and with shadowboxing for speed and technique. For the same reason as headbutts, they're a little tricky to use when sparring, especially for elbows. One solution to that problem would be to wear elbow pads if you so choose. Whatever you decide, you can't afford not to add them to your weekly practice. Not if you plan to become deadlier than 99% of the population.

Grappling Techniques: Time for a Nap/Break

This book wouldn't be complete without a quick section on chokes and locks. Even if they clearly won't be our bread and butter as: a) their uses are highly more restricted than our dear kicks and punches which we can deliver from various distances and in almost any position; b) they require that you get a hold of your opponent (which is sometimes harder to do than to just rain punches down on his face); they can still be of use when, for example, we need to control someone until a law enforcement officer decides to show up.

As always, we'll only learn the most efficient and versatile of them.

Choking Techniques

Before we start, forget everything you "think" you know about chokes. Yes, in movies, the hero can kill his enemy by simply wrapping an arm around his neck. Yes, in movies, the villain often resorts to a double-hand choke to squeeze the throat of poor, defenseless women and strangle them.

But like I said, forget about this.

For one, we're not trying to put our adversaries out of their misery yet but to put them to sleep. Anyway, you can't kill someone by just choking him for a few seconds. Chokes work by stopping the flow of oxygen to the brain. Rendering people unconscious is what they do and what we seek. Now, you could possibly send someone off to meet his maker but you would have to keep the choke down long after he would have ceased to offer any resistance. To cause irreversible damage to the brain (akin to killing that person), you would have to deprive it from oxygen for more than 6 minutes. I hope you'll never have to resort to such extreme measures.

As for that double-hand choke I mentioned earlier, c'mon now! They don't come as lousy as that one. Not only is it highly ineffective as you're using your fingers to press down on that neck – which means that, unless you're a Captain of Crush Hall of Famer who managed to close the No.4 gripper, you won't have enough strength in your hands to do anything but make the opponent burst out with laughter –, you will also leave your entire body open to strikes.

Now that we've gotten that out of the way, let's review some of the most famous chokes:

- **The triangle choke**: though this move looks extremely nice, we can make no exception here. It must suffer the same fate as our beloved jumping kicks. This ain't the UFC where you can be thrown to the floor and work a nice submission from your back. If you get slammed on concrete, you won't be able to remember your name, so you can imagine your chances of pulling that complicated maneuver off. Therefore, to our huge dismay, it must get the no-go;
- **The guillotine choke**: this choke, on the other hand, can be extremely useful. It's not too technical and it can be locked pretty quickly when your aggressor charges and leaves his neck free for the taking. Just wrap that head under one arm and clasp your hands together so that your hands are now pressing against his trachea. Lean back and drive your fists into his neck to cut the air supply and send that bad boy take a nap (watch out for groin strikes);

- **The rear-naked choke**: if you've got siblings, you've probably already dealt or been on the receiving end of this powerful choke as a kid. All you got to do to perform a rear-naked is take your opponent's back, which isn't as hard as you might think if you've been working on your speed and can surprise him by slipping behind, slide one arm under his chin, grab your other forearm with that hand, and squeeze tight while pulling your hips backwards. Most people have no clue as to how to defend against this choke; so, it will usually go smooth as silk.

Locking Techniques

Breakin' and poppin' may be a great style of street dance but it's also a brutal way to end a fight. Locks are supposed to give you control over the adversary and render him harmless by breaking his limbs and making him unable to fight back.

At least, that's the theory. I found out that, in practice, compared to strikes and chokes, they don't play that decisive a role (especially when standing.) Locks are at their best when grappling on the floor and, with reduced mobility on both sides, you can isolate an arm or an ankle and rip it off more easily. When you're on your two feet and you seize a joint to twist it, not only will the other guy have ample time to pull back and free himself from the hold, you'll be abandoning all defense as with the lousy 2 handed choke we talked about.

Then, why not take the fight to the ground? After all, isn't it true that 90% of street fights end up on the ground anyway? I don't know about those statistics (has anyone ever really studied the subject?) but if some fights do end up on the floor, it's rarely intentional. It's often because one of the two fighters got sucker punched and fell down, and the other fellow just followed him there to finish his work. It's almost never a tactical play to try and work a kimura, for example.

In my opinion, it's never smart to trade your standing stance in a hostile environment where you never know what might happen next. Once on the ground, you're far more vulnerable to other guys stepping in and starting to kick or stomp you. You can't run away either if need be. The best way to approach a fight is to just deal with the threat and get out of there before possible back-up arrives. Working a proper submission takes too much time and preparation. We can't afford to play chess here; we need to go fast and hard. Use the hammer over the precision tools, if you will...

Believe me, I love arm bars and omoplatas, but your time will be better spent elsewhere, training your speed and your hips for example. The only lock I would recommend learning is a simple hammerlock as performed by the police, for those few instances where you need to immobilize someone or keep him in check until you've escorted him out of some place. To do a hammerlock, you need to grab one of your opponent's arms and force it up his back. You can also decide to add some extra pressure by squeezing at the wrist at the same time. When performing that lock, use your other arm to control the head and avoid headbutts from the back of his skull. Press with your forearm down on his neck.

Now, if you truly want to learn chokes and locks in all their subtleties, I won't try to dissuade you, but remember that you can't become a master of everything by playing the jack of all trades. At some point, if we don't want to train 15 hours a week, we have to draw a line in the sand and choose the best bang for our buck. And as far as I'm concerned, that will always be striking moves.

Fair Play/Foul Play? On the Value of Abiding to a Code

As Superheroes in training, we might come to think that we need to stick to certain rules when dealing with a foe. After all, even if we need to kick butt, we're still here to make an example, right? To serve as an example. Thus, we ought to deal with the situation like any other, that is with ethics and integrity.

If that's what you think, I applaud you. I wish things were that easy, that people behaved like the samurai from ancient times, with dignity and honor. But you'll quickly see that the thugs of today have more in common with Judas than with those noble warriors. You'll see that your pious wishes will get thrown out the window the second your opponent pokes you in the eye or tries to bite your ear off. I know, you two were supposed to keep it honorable... Unfortunately, it doesn't happen that way in real life.

This is not a sanctioned competition or some orchestrated Kung fu choreography. Things can get ugly real quick, so you need to know the truth not only to be able to defend against cheap shots but also because, sometimes, you might have to resort to them to save you!

Always Strike First

Whenever possible, I would suggest you try and defuse the conflict before it has a chance to escalate. Sometimes, a bit of diplomacy can go a long way and avoid a lot of unnecessary violence and hospital bills. But some other times, all the other party will understand is a good punch to the face.

When things start to unravel and a fight seems unavoidable, always be the first to strike. Don't wait for the adversary to engage and risk losing the upper hand. In a fight situation, it's never good to react. You must act and be decisive in your moves. Hit quick and hit hard. As they say, the best form of defense is attack.

With luck, you'll end the fight right there. That's the best case scenario as you need to be aware that the longer you two keep fighting, the riskier it gets for you.

This is where the headbutt can prove invaluable. When the opponent gets in your face and starts threatening you, as soon as you see him make the slightest gesture, throw a headbutt in his nose. 9 times out of 10, you'll catch him off-guard and you'll only have to follow with a quick hands combination to seal the deal. Never underestimate the element of surprise when you're the first to attack.

The problem we face is in determining when exactly to engage and when it's better to just hold off. You see, being the one to throw the first punch exposes you to potential legal action later on. So you need to make sure you have absolutely no other choice. You must be certain there's no other way to get out of this tight spot unharmed.

To help you gauge the situation, here are 2 things to watch out for more specifically:

- **The distance between you and your opponent**: is the adversary keeping at a safe distance or is he walking towards you? Is he within punching range? The closer he gets, the more dangerous the situation. Warn him not to come closer and see if he continues to move forward. If he does, get ready to initiate contact;
- **The opponent's non-verbal communication**: if what the adversary says is important, it's the non-verbal cues you'll want to pay special attention to. That's what will allow you to judge whether he's just muttering empty threats like those small doggies that bark louder than they bite or if he's ready to pounce on you like a rabid pitbull. Watch those hands at all times. That's where the danger almost always comes from; whether it's a weapon he draws out of his pocket or a punch he arms back to throw at your face. Be warned that not everyone will be shaking and walking with tensed shoulders and clenched fists when they're about to assault you, though. Some guys will approach you, calm and collected, until they sucker punch you or dive their head right into your poor cheekbone. Those are the nastiest, those you must keep an eye out for. That's why you need to remain in control of your surroundings and not let anyone get too close without making them pay right away.

Fighting Dirty

When your life is on the line, like I said, there are no more rules. Why take a deliberate handicap and start at a serious disadvantage when the guy who's trying to put you down and out has recourse to every dirty trick in the book?

If I can finish him with a good old cross-hook combination or a knee to the solar plexus, I'll do it. But if he's really trying to hurt me or threatens to harm someone I care about, I may leave his jaw be and rather focus on the following spots:

- **The eyes**: this is an instant fight stopper. It usually doesn't take more than a simple poke to one eye to cause a sharp and immediate pain. You'll see your opponent blink as if a pound of sand had blown into his eyes. The risk with attacking the eyes is to cause a detachment of the retina or to induce permanent blindness if you go too hard;
- **The groin**: if you're a guy, you know what a pain it is to get hit there. So, if the situation justifies it, knee or soccer-kick your adversary in the groin. He won't be putting much of a fight afterwards as he'll be too busy dealing with the horrendous abdominal pain that comes with it. You can also choose to punch him in that area if you've lost your balance and fell on one knee. The risk with attacking the groin is to cause testicular torsion and jeopardize your adversary's fertility. You may even break the pubic bone as a bonus. Double ouch!
- **The throat and the neck**: the neck is a highly vulnerable area in that you have both the oxygen and the blood passing through. While you need to apply a successful choke to prevent the blood from irrigating the brain, you won't have to go to such trouble for disrupting the air influx. A quick jab to the windpipe will often suffice to bring your adversary to his knees, gasping for air. You also have the cervical vertebrae at the back which can be targeted with elbows. The risk with attacking the neck and the throat is severe, even more so than with the groin. You could collapse the throat and kill that person or cripple him for the rest of his days. Not cool. To be used as a very last resort;
- **The knees**: knees can be struck with front kicks when the opponent leaves one leg out straight in front of him. By hitting the kneecap with the ball of your foot, you can dislocate the joint and restrict his ability to move. With sufficient power, you might even break the knee;
- **The collarbone**: an easier bone to break, the clavicle will give in if you manage to hit it right on. Knees in the clinch are especially good to target that small area. With a broken collarbone, your opponent won't be able to use his arm effectively anymore. No serious complications involved, so no remorse in using this technique…;
- **The ears**: last but not least, if I don't recommend you go all Mike Tyson on your adversary and make a feast of his earlobe, you can still aim for his ears with a good open palm smack. That should disorient him and have him lose his balance.

Using the Environment to Your Advantage

Fights can break out at anytime and anywhere. I would even go so far as to say that they often happen when you expect them the least. You're waiting for the bus with your girlfriend when some jerk starts hitting on her and making some inappropriate comments. You tell him to leave you alone but, instead of listening to you, that guy turns on you and becomes threatening. What do you do?

You're not at the dojo or in a ring. This is not a controlled environment that was especially thought out and created to ensure the safety of a fighter. You have no flexible ropes to welcome your weight if you fall back. No soft mat underneath your feet to save you, should you end up on the floor. What you do have though are items lying around that can be used as improvised weapons and people potentially waiting in ambush!

In this type of scenario, you need to assess the situation quickly to determine where the danger may lie but also to decide on the best course of action to take. In a street fight, your actions will always be affected by your surroundings.

Be Aware of Your Surroundings

First question to answer: can you get out of there quickly if things get out of hand?

In our example, you could take your girl by the arm, say to hell with it, and walk to the next stop. You're in the open; so, unless something is blocking your way or the other guy starts following you, you could avoid coming to blows by simply leaving (I know this option isn't the most glamorous as it would seem like you're fleeing your tail between your legs, but learning to be better than most also means becoming smarter and realizing that every conflict doesn't require that you step up and express your virility with your fists. You won't win anything but a free pass to the police station.)

It's always nice to have the luxury of choosing between fight or flight, especially when the danger becomes increasingly apparent and you might suddenly need to sprint the heck out of there to save your skin. That's why, as soon as a threat comes up on your radar, take the habit of looking around to weigh your alternatives. Just in case. Try and spot the different exit points, which routes would provide the quickest escape and which could prove more challenging. When facing a massive opponent who might not be as agile as you, that high fence a hundred feet to your left might be the perfect option. If you're inside a building, what doors are the nearest and what windows could you possibly use to perform your vanishing act?

In case you're a long way from home, in a place you don't know much about, and the guy who's after you seems to hold a strong grudge and won't let you get away that easily – or if you're on foot and being chased by a car –, can you find anything that might serve as a temporary hiding spot? Anything that could provide some cover until the heat drops?

If your eyes must scan around you for possible getaways, they should also pay attention to what you're standing on. What type of surface lies under you? Is it hard, soft? Is it stable, unstable? Dry or wet and slippery? Maybe there are gravels or some sand that could be thrown to the opponent's face to blind him? One of the reasons you should inspect your surroundings is to figure out what objects might be used against you and what you could take advantage of to attack or defend yourself. Items like a glass you could smash on someone's skull, an iron bar to play ball with his knees or a chair to keep him at bay.

Every element in your vicinity may ultimately help or be used against you. Even the weather. So always be aware of your surroundings.

Environmental Training

As you've seen, the terrain you find yourself on may play a huge role in how the situation eventually unfolds. What does that mean as far your training is concerned? Well, it means you will gain a huge edge over your adversaries by taking your sessions outside and practicing your moves in all kinds of different settings. This will get you used to keeping your balance on wobbly floors, to not being distracted by the rain or the fierce blows of the wind in your face.

Most fighters only train indoors, in the comfort of their club. Once they lose contact with the familiar feeling of the tatami under their feet, they seem to completely lose their bearings. They don't know how to react anymore, as if everything they had learned and trained for did not apply in the outside world. They let the circumstances take the better of them and claim, afterwards, that it was because of the weather they got their head smashed in or because they had no room to move. The truth is that they just weren't ready! It was their fault and their fault alone.

Don't let that be you. Train wherever and at any time of day or night, so when the time comes, it'll be the other guy who'll have to make up excuses as to why he got beat up so bad. Also, don't make the mistake of always training with the same outfit. Fighting in a pair of jeans and a jacket is a lot different than with wide shorts that offer great amplitude of motion. Get used to punching and kicking in your everyday clothes. Once again, it's all about preparing for anything.

Fighting Multiple Opponents

Fighting one man can already be troublesome but having to hold your own against two or more earns maximum points on the suckiness scale. As the number of assailants increases so does your risk of incurring serious injuries if not death! You know, I'm always one to joke and to take things lightly, but facing numerous attackers sure is no laughing matter!

Several opponents equal double, triple, if not 4 times as many limbs to keep an eye on and to defend against. No matter your level of proficiency, if you don't stop the threat fast and for good, you're going to get overwhelmed before you had a chance to say your last words. If you can anticipate the attacks from your adversary when fighting 1-on-1 by focusing on his moves, it's impossible to do that with a handful guys hopping around like vultures around a dying calf. You can't protect your entire body when blows start pouring down from every direction. So what are you to do?

Minimizing the Numerical Advantage

One of the best ways to survive such an encounter is to look for ways to reduce the number of opponents to fight at the same time. Your ultimate goal, if you can't escape the scene, would be to take on each one of them separately.

Here are a few techniques that can help:

- **Taunting**: despite what I said earlier about showing diplomacy and not doing anything to aggravate the situation, in this case trash-talking may work at your advantage. If you can isolate the leader of the pack and have him (and not his entire crew) fight you by putting his honor on the line, you've already won. Ask him if he really needs his friends to beat you, if he's got that small a pair of b**** that he doesn't dare to take you on *mano a mano*. Sometimes, you'll even hear his friends pressing him to accept the challenge after that;
- **Be bold**: you can walk up to the first guy, slap him. Then go to the next one, raise your hand and squeeze it into a tight fist, and ask him if he wants one too. Both techniques, "taunting" and "being bold", work by demonstrating your extreme confidence and instilling doubt in your adversary's mind. But they won't achieve anything against real life predators who're looking for

something else than a little trouble or street credit. Against people aiming to rob or hurt you personally, you'll be better off using one of the 2 following tips;

- **Running**: sprinting isn't just a great avoidance technique not to get hurt, it can also be used to isolate your enemies one from another. If the space around you allows, start dashing for a few hundred meters to scatter your pursuers apart. All of a sudden, turn around and surprise the nearest with a swift blow;
- **Using the environment**: this is an application of my previous tip to make the setting work for you. If possible, try and maneuver your adversaries into a narrow line so they'll be forced to wait their turn to take their shot at you. Corridors, alleys but also rows of tables can help to block the sides and protect your most vulnerable areas.

Show No Mercy

I can understand you may want to keep the fight respectable when facing one adversary and avoid the cheap shots. But when cowards team up to get an unfair advantage, keep your kindness for people who deserve it. This sort of situation calls for nothing short of your worst violence and wrath.

When you've tried everything to prevent a showdown and it's now only a matter of seconds before a fight erupts, you must show no hesitation. If they strike first, you're done. More than ever, here, be the one to launch the attack. Strike to hurt and disable. Appeal to every dirty trick you know of; aim for the groin, the eyes, the throat and the knees.

Your life truly is at risk, so leave nothing to chance. Swarm those boys in such a way that they'll forever regret ever messing with you, and don't stop going until they either flee or find themselves on the floor, out and cold.

One big problem when dealing with 3 or more assailants is to watch out not to gas too quickly because, once you're out of breath, your speed will drop dramatically. And you know what that means, right? Your opponents will be on you like a wolf pack on a juicy steak. It's even more problematic that you must go hard and throw everything you've got in your attacks to try and end it all up as fast as possible, which can quickly burn you out.

This stresses the critical importance of building a strong cardio! Getting tired in a fight is not only one of the worst feelings ever, it's also highly dangerous when there's no referee around to come to the rescue. Controlling your breathing will thus ensure you can go the distance but also that you keep a sharp mind and not let your emotions or the adrenalin take over.

In short, the key to survival in a fight against multiple opponents is to show no mercy. To be brutal and relentless.

Defending against Weapons

I'll be quick here as there's not much to say anyway. I know there's a gazillion books out there that claim to teach you how to neutralize an armed opponent and take the upper hand. They show you all types of crazy moves like disarming a guy holding a gun by immobilizing the hand around the handle and turning it against its owner. Yeah, right! That's the kind of behavior that will only get you killed faster than a hedgehog on a busy interstate!

I can help you develop a tough skin that should be able to withstand any punch or knee. But, unfortunately, I still haven't discovered the secret to turning it to steel like Colossus and taking a bullet and smile about it.

What about knives? Contrary to intuition, they're not safer than firearms in close combat by a long shot. They can slash, pierce, tear apart... One strike to the wrong area and you might bleed to your death. My only piece of advice when it comes to facing armed opponents would be not to even try to resist! Get out of there! There's no shame in running away when the odds are stacked against you and the game was rigged from the start.

If your back is against the wall and you can't take your leave, try and find something to protect you or to keep the attacker at a distance. Anything. It could be the lid of a trashcan, a broom or even your jacket that you could wrap around your arm to avoid getting cut. With weapons, the risk is just too high to be tempting fate. Fighting is a tool to keep you alive and well. Don't use it as the shovel to dig your own grave!

PART VI

The 100 Days Program
to Make a Killer out of You!

"*You can prep for a field mission all you want.
But if working in a lab has taught me one thing...
It's that theory and practice are radically
different concepts.*"

Ant-Man

Alright, buddy! This is where we lay it all down. This is where we get serious, roll up our sleeves and detail our training program for the next 100 days.

In a way, this is the most important part of this entire book. Without it, you wouldn't change a bit. In fact, you could read everything that's ever been written on the topic of fighting, if you don't take action at some point, you won't see any more difference in your life than the poor office clerk who dreams of hitting big and reads volume after volume of "how to get rich" schemes but never finds the power in himself to start applying any of them.

I hope you'll realize that knowledge without action is as useful to you as a seesaw without any teeth. That if you are to become tougher, deadlier and more fearless than 99% of the population, you had better move your butt and put your money where your mouth is!

As I explained in the previous book, my training plans last 100 days because that's how long it takes to form new habits. But also because you'll need that much time for the brain-muscle connections to strengthen and for you to become proficient with your new moves. Although it usually takes years to master regular martial arts, by focusing on what really matters and ditching the superfluous, you'll be able to reach a high level in no time.

Obviously, you'll want to carry on working on your strikes and defense after these 100 days, in order to continue improving your power, your speed, your precision and your stamina. However, you'll have fulfilled the contract and you should be able by then to stand up to anyone and hold your own without any problem! After that, every new progress will just be a bonus.

Week 01 - Week 04

During our first month, our top priority will be to work on the basics and drill them until they become second nature. We will focus on technique over speed and power to ensure we got the moves down perfect before we add any more level of difficulty (remember that it's much harder to correct a technique than it is to learn it!)

If you've read any of my previous work, you know I'm a huge proponent of progressive methods. No point in trying to juggle 10 different balls at the same time. All we'd get out of it would be busted feet and a whole lot of frustration. Training in increments is the best way to prepare your body and not only avoid injury but also guarantee the best results possible by building a strong enough basis to be able to develop our other skills and aptitudes later on. With weak foundations, you'll never rise above the pack and obtain the edge to prevail at all times. So, keep it simple, Superboy!

For this first cycle, we'll be training 3 times a week. I'll let you decide on which days you prefer to work out but I would recommend you space your sessions by at least 1 day to make sure you give your body enough time to recover. It'll be especially important when strengthening your fists as your skin needs time to heal and toughen up.

But first things first, how are we going to arrange those training sessions? What are we going to drill, when and for how long?

All in all, you should rarely spend much more than an hour working out on any of those days. There's just no need to. If you train hard and train smart, you'll achieve your goals without you having to jeopardize your social life or all your free time.

We'll start each one of those sessions with a light warm-up. We'll kill 2 birds with 1 stone by using a jumping rope to get the sweat going. It will allow us to work on our footwork at the same time. If you've never skipped rope before, don't get discouraged if you can't align 2 jumps in a row. It's one of those things that you just have to "get", and once you do, it'll be like child's play. Usually, after a few days of practice, you should have found your rhythm. Don't worry about speed or doing crazy moves like double-unders or crossed jumps yet. You should aim for smoothness and being as light on your feet as can be.

You will jump for a grand total of 10 minutes. You can rest every now and then to catch your breath or to relax your arms if you feel you need to but, eventually, you'll want to jump the entire time without stopping.

Once you're sufficiently warm and you've prepared your joints with some rotations and slight stretching, you'll continue working on your footwork as you practice your stance. Footwork is a tricky beast, so the sooner you start taming it, the sooner you'll get control over it.

In front of a mirror, if you can, start practicing moving around with your guard up. Get used to bouncing off the balls of your feet and being like Ali's butterfly. Don't throw any strike yet. Just focus on your feet and moving in and out, going to the side. Pay attention never to let your guard down. This will serve to teach your body to always have your hands in protection when you move. Do this for another 10 minutes

After that will come technique training. Like I said, when you're in the first stages of your evolution, it's good to reduce every punch and kick to their bare essentials. So, for our attacks, we will start drilling them while standing still. You already have much to think about to ensure perfect motion, so don't overcomplicate things by having to watch your footwork as well while learning your strikes.

This section will consist in 8 rounds of 3 minutes (and 1 minute of rest in between), divided as such:

- 2 rounds of straight punches (nothing but jabs and crosses);
- 1 round of hooks;
- 1 round of uppercuts;
- 2 rounds of kicks (low and middle kicks + front kicks);
- 2 rounds of mixing it up (use simple 1-2, 1-2-3 combos like the double-jab, the double-jab-straight, the jab-straight and left hook, the jab-straight and leg kick, the right-cross-left-hook);

In short, nothing too fancy yet. This is about teaching your body the proper movements and learning how to transition smoothly between techniques. That's why I cannot insist enough on the importance of going slow. Don't throw everything you've got into your punches just yet. Focus on making every one of them a true piece of art. Watch yourself in the mirror to correct your form, as I recommended. Better yet, record yourself with a camera or your phone so you can review your moves later on and compare with videos of professional fighters.

Another important part of this program is conditioning. If you've gone through the 100 days of volume 01, you should already have enough gas in your tank to outlast anyone. You know what you're doing, so continue with your current cardio practice.

If you haven't, add 10 minutes of HIIT to the end of your session. I'm not going to explain once again the many benefits of high intensity interval training; you'll have to take my word for it. Let's just say that, in a fight, you need to be able to go at max speed and intensity for short periods of time. That's why HIIT is so beneficial as it emulates the very conditions of a fight. On the other hand, running long distances at a leisurely pace won't help much as we're not trying to prepare ourselves for 1 hour snorefests!

When I talk about conditioning, there's the cardio aspect but also the body strengthening side of it. For these first few weeks, we will go light and do fist push-ups on a soft surface like a carpet or a folded towel. As for the neck and the abs, work them right after (3sets of 10reps.)

Flexibility exercises will conclude our sessions with 10 minutes of stretching the legs and the lower back.

Also, don't forget to take your training outside once a week to get used to different types of weather and grounds. Get out and go smell the flowers; it'll change from the odors of sweat at your regular place. And use different clothing.

Last but not least, every night, when you go to sleep and close your eyes, use visualization techniques to help cement your resolve. Go through the scenarios I talked about. Imagine yourself kicking butt and taking names. Imagine yourself a great fearless warrior, and that's what you'll become!

Week 05 - Week 09

Good job, so far. We're now 1 month in and you should have already improved by leaps and bounds. While I wouldn't yet label you the new Floyd Mayweather of punching and kicking, striking should almost come natural to you. You should have passed that awkward moment where you don't know what to do with your 4 limbs. It's thus time to pick up speed.

First, we will add movements to our shadowboxing. Not just the feet but the torso as well as we start practicing dodging techniques. The main goal of this coming month, though, will be to increase our striking speed. We will also learn how to properly use our knees and elbows.

So how does that all translate into our training sessions? Every time we work out, during these next weeks, we'll stick to the following routine:

- **Warm-up**: 10 minutes of jumping rope (mix different techniques);
- **Shadowboxing**: 5x3min rounds of working your strikes and footwork. Focus on your speed. Be in and out like the wind;
- **Technique**: as you did last month with the basic attacks, work your elbows and knees slowly. Add some dodging here and there. 2 rounds of elbows, 2 rounds of knees;

- **Sparring**: if you've got a partner to train with, start sparring for 2 or 3 rounds of 2 minutes. Go light and slower than usual to train your eye to see the attacks coming;
- **Conditioning**: mix speed ladder drills with your regular HIIT sessions to keep things fresh and your body guessing (10 minutes) + take your fist push-ups to a harder surface and continue working that neck and those abs;
- **Flexibility**: same as the previous month.

We'll still go outside and take our breath of fresh air once a week.

What I also like to do, even if it makes me look like some kind of psycho to people who might see me, is to randomly throw rapid combinations throughout the day. I'll be walking my dog and, suddenly, burst into a cross, left hook, leg kick combo. This helps further strengthening the neural connections.

At night, use your visualization techniques and make sure to breathe from the belly.

Week 10 - Week 15

After the 2 months mark, that's where people usually see their motivation drop. They lose track of what initially inspired them to start and find themselves having to combat their lethargy with all their might because there's just not much drive behind them anymore. Don't let that be you. Use your visualization techniques to always remind yourself why you're doing all this.

For week 10 to week 15, we will introduce you to power training. I know, it was about time! We will also begin working on our reflexes, as well as our chokes and locks if you've got someone at hand to torture and put to sleep.

The main tool we'll be using here is the heavy bag. Now, I'm not going to demand or urge you to buy one if it's not within your means but, if it's no big deal for you, I would heartily suggest you spend the cash as a good bag will be worth every cent.

If you can't afford to buy one, you'll have to show some ingenuity and build one. Use stuff that's lying around like piles of tires or a duffel bag you can fill with old rags and pieces of fabric. There's not much equipment needed to progress with my training methods but, to develop serious power, a bag is one of the few absolute must.

I would add a 4th weekly session for the next 5 weeks if that's doable on your side as we have a lot to work on, but I'll leave that up to you and your schedule (3 sessions a week is still great, so no worries if you can't make up time for a fourth.)

Alright, enough with the speeches. Without further ado, here's the plan for the third and final month:

- **Warm-up**: 10 minutes of jumping rope (mix different techniques);
- **Shadowboxing**: 4x3min rounds of working your strikes (all the moves, from the jab to the knees), dodging techniques and footwork. Once again, make it all about speed;
- **Power training**: for your bag work, keep it simple. Choose one basic combination (like a jab, right cross) that you will drill for an entire round of 3 minutes. Pause between every repetition and,

when you go for it, rotate those hips to the max and try to punch a hole in that bag. Aim for 5 rounds and switch techniques in between;

- **Sparring**: if you've got a partner, spar for 3 rounds of 3 minutes. Increase the speed and power compared to last month to make you comfortable with the idea of punching someone in the face and getting hit in return;
- **Reflexes**: depending on the equipment you got on hand, you will either use mitts, the maize or the double ended bag to work your timing. If all else fails, train your range like I explained in Part III by stopping your attacks half an inch from a designated target. 3x3min rounds;
- **Conditioning**: HIIT for 10 minutes + condition your fists by hitting that bag with the least amount of protection you can afford + train the abs and have your partner land some light shots to your stomach for desensitization purposes;
- **Flexibility**: by now, you should have completely opened your hips if you trained seriously. To get yet closer to the full split, I would focus on the straddle stretch. Sit in the position, grab a good book and keep the tension in the legs for as long as you want/can.

Every now and then, include some speed work at the heavy bag where you will hit it as fast as possible for 20 seconds straight and rest twice that time before going with another round. Make it your speed training for that day.

And there you have it: my 100 days program to make a bad*** out of you! Well, that's the theory anyway. To get there and change your life, you still have to put it all into practice!

That's why, if I were you, I wouldn't think too much about it and just start right away. Don't wait for doubt or the tentacles of procrastination to come and ruin it all. You need to act when you still got a chance and build up momentum. Don't let this book end up like so many other training guides which provide a good reading experience but eventually find their way into a library where they'll collect dust until, some years later, you stumble back upon them and wonder what could have been if you had used their information.

Let this be the start of a new chapter. Let it work for you, so you can become tougher and free yourself from your fears. Your dreams of greatness are within reach. All you've got to do is reach out and grab them! Good luck.

Let's Keep in Touch

Now that this book comes to an end, I'd like to extend a hand to you. I feel like we're somehow connected now. I hope that the content of this guide resonated with you and your past experiences, that you could identify with my journey, my ambitions and setbacks. If that's the case, no matter where you are in life today, we're kindred spirits with yet a lot to share!

That's why I'd like to keep in touch; so we can continue to progress together. We've both embarked on a road that knows no end, a road to perfection that can sometimes get very lonely when no one else around you can relate. We can offer each other that support. We can help each other become better!

Whether you have a question to ask, a comment or suggestion you'd like to make, or if you simply want to tell me about your goals and the progress you've already made, you can reach me:

Via my site: http:reallifesuperman.com

Or on my personal email address: markus@reallifesuperman.com

It'll be my pleasure to help!

Speaking of help, if you have 2 minutes to spare, I'd like to ask for yours. I need your feedback to find out if I'm on the right track. I've tried to lay down everything I know about the fighting game but it's still a work in progress. I know it can still be improved. That's why I'd like to hear what you have to say about it. If you could do me a favor and drop a word or two about this book on Amazon, it would mean the world to me!

I thank you in advance and I'll see you soon, my friend.

About the Author

A black belt in Karate, ring-tested kickboxer who also holds a university degree in Psychology, I have to admit I know a thing or two about kicking butt and imposing my will on my foes. However, the real adversary I've always been looking to vanquish – whether in CrossFit competitions, in a race or a fight – has never been anyone else but me.

I believe in the Latin phrase *mens sana in corpore sano* and try to honor that spirit every chance I get by looking for new, more efficient ways to improve myself and reach the next level. Through my trials and errors, I've accumulated a vast wealth of knowledge. Not only on the **quickest means to attain one's physical peak** but also on what it takes to **toughen up mentally and develop a sharp, indestructible mind**.

In this series of books, I intend to share with you everything I've learned in close to 20 years of studying and perfecting my training. It is the next natural step for me: to put into words all that baggage made of sensations, hard-earned habits and unspoken truths; to extract its very essence without holding anything back. And by so doing, not only will I get better, you will as well!

Some of the facts I'll lay out will surprise you, others may come as a shock, but rest assured that they represent the **fastest shortcut to success**. So, if you're ready for the change of a lifetime, let's get started and discover the Superhero who had been hiding inside you all along!

Sincerely,

45815723R00057

Made in the USA
Lexington, KY
11 October 2015